ID0787373

# Mississippians

SECOND EDITION

Edited by Neil White

Copyright © 2011 by The Nautilus Publishing Company
One Town Square Lane, Suite 5 • P.O. Box 40 • Taylor, Mississippi 38673
Tel: 662-513-0159 • Fax: 662-234-9266 • www.Mississippians.com
www.nautiluspublishing.com

To order bulk copies for educational or corporate use, call 662-513-0159 or email info@nautiluspublishing.com

PRINTED IN CHINA BY EVERBEST PRINTING COMPANY LTD
through an arrangement with Four Colour Print Group, Louisville, Kentucky

# The Inspiration for *Mississippians*

I love to encounter strangers who know little of our state — especially those who believe the oversimplified, often sensationalized, reports about Mississippi. Nothing is quite as gratifying as rattling off a list of notable, accomplished Mississippians. I start with football: the greatest receiver of all time; the most prolific quarterback of all time; the most admired running back of all time. Then I move to literature: the greatest novelist of the 20th century; the best playwright of the 20th century; the best-selling author in America; more Pulitzer Prize winners per capita than any other state. Then on to music: the King of Rock and Roll; the King of the Blues; the men who inspired the rock and roll movement. Next, film and television: the most beloved actor of our generation; the most powerful woman in entertainment; and the two most recognizable narrative voices in the world. I usually finish the onslaught with the founder of FedEx; the founder of MTV; the man who introduced Netscape to the world.

Then I ask: "Would you like to compare lists?"

## What Makes a Mississippian?

For purposes of this book, we define Mississippians as anyone who was born in the state, who made Mississippi home, who attended one of Mississippi's colleges or universities, or who spent a significant portion of his or her life in the state.

## Just the Beginning

*Mississippians* showcases our extraordinary citizens through the lenses and pens of some our state's top writers and photographers. But we are just beginning. We will expand and update the publication periodically. We realize hundreds of Mississippians living exceptional lives are waiting to be photographed and profiled. And we know that extraordinary Mississippians are yet to be discovered.

You may nominate Mississippians at *www.Mississippians.com* or by e-mail at *info@mississippians.com*.

We hope you enjoy this glimpse into Mississippi as much as we have enjoyed the process of publishing the expanded second edition. We look forward to hearing from you. And, in my future, I look forward to handing this book to strangers — rather than subject them to my rants.

Neil White, *Editor*

# ICONIC MISSISSIPPIANS

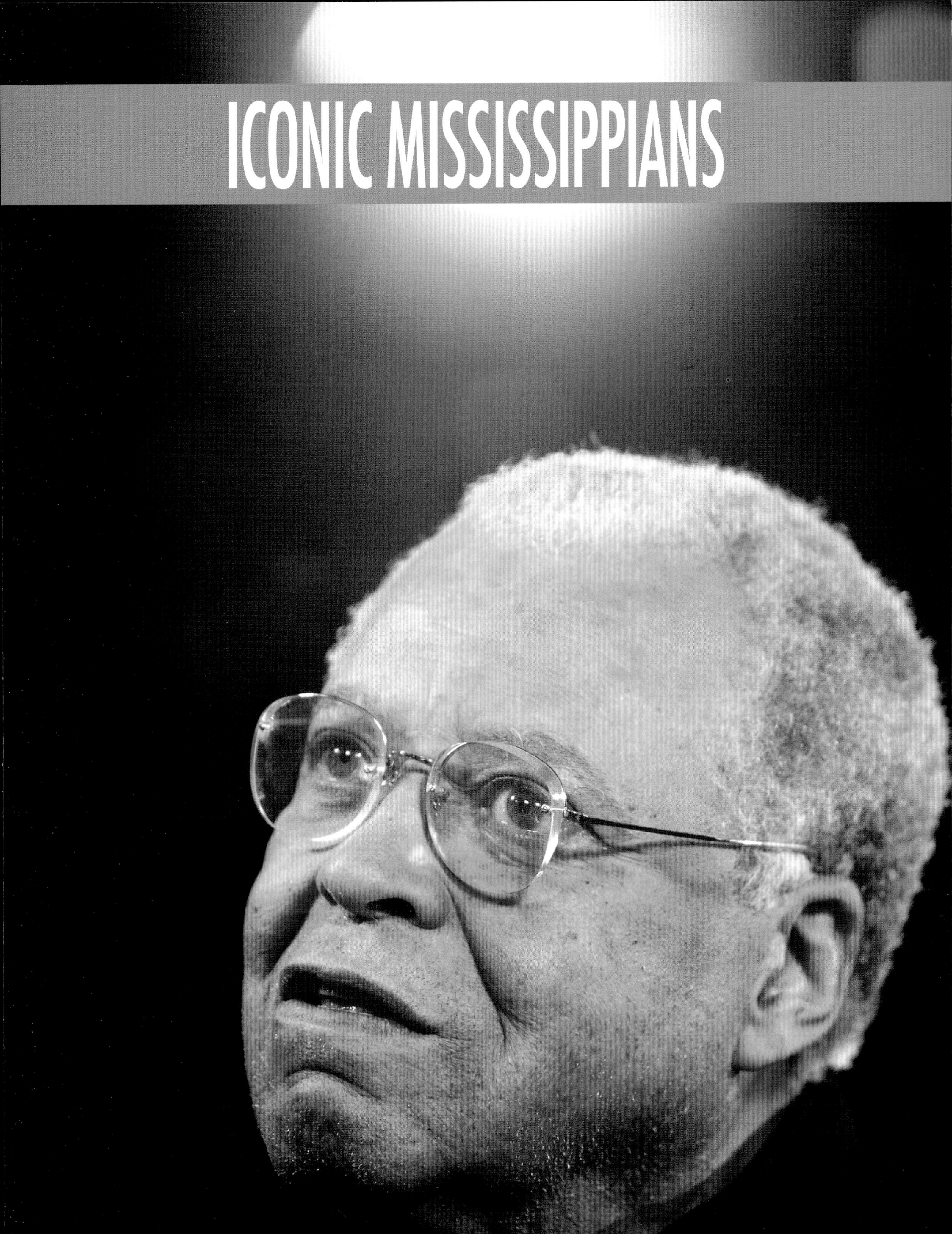

# ELVIS PRESLEY

**"Before Elvis, there was nothing."**
*John Lennon*

It started out like any other Saturday outing to the Tupelo Hardware Store. The boy wanted a gun. His mother suggested a bike. They spotted a guitar on the wall and struck a compromise. The rest is history.

Elvis Aaron Presley is one of the most important pop-culture figures of the 20th Century. In 1958, Elvis accounted for more than 50 percent of the sales of RCA Records. He had more number-one songs than any performer before him. His forty-plus movies were all Hollywood hits. Worldwide record sales exceeded one billion.

No one could have predicted Elvis' success. Growing up, he lived in a public housing complex in Memphis, he was bullied for being a "mama's boy," and a high school music teacher once told him: "You have no aptitude for singing."

But Elvis' dedication to his mother paid off. In August of 1953, he walked into the offices of Sun Records in Memphis to record a song for his mom's birthday. There he met Sam Phillips, who had been looking for a white singer to bring the sound of black music to the masses.

Phillips turned out to be a visionary. And we can all cherish the memory of Elvis grabbing a microphone and belting out: "You ain't nothing but a hound dog."

**Photograph**  Rock and roll singer Elvis Presley poses for a portrait on a movie set circa 1960 in Los Angeles, California.
Photo by Michael Ochs Archives/Getty Images

# OPRAH WINFREY

**"Understand that the right to choose your own path is a
sacred privilege. Use it. Dwell in possibility."**

*Oprah Winfrey*

Oprah Winfrey was so poor as a child, she wore a dress made out of a potato sack. The daughter of teenage parents from Kosciusko, Mississippi, Oprah's life could have been another tragic tale of poverty. But her grandmother intervened. She taught Oprah to read — before Oprah turned three. She emphasized the importance of education. She took Oprah to church.

Oprah was an honor student who excelled in speech, and she landed a job at a radio station while still in high school. Her conversational style led to a series of talk shows. And on September 8, 1986, *The Oprah Winfrey Show* was broadcast for the first time nationally.

Oprah's work isn't restricted to daytime television. Her film credits include *The Color Purple, Beloved, Charlotte's Web*, and *The Princess and the Frog*. She has co-authored five books. Her magazine, *O*, is the most successful magazine start-up in history. And her work as a philanthropist is unparalleled.

Oprah is, without a doubt, the most influential woman in entertainment. *Time* magazine called her "the world's most powerful woman." Her new television network, *OWN*, was launched in 2011.

Before 1986, no one outside of Mississippi had ever heard of Oprah Winfrey. Now, there's no need for the last name. Oprah is recognized worldwide.

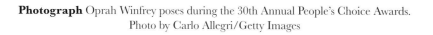

**Photograph** Oprah Winfrey poses during the 30th Annual People's Choice Awards.
Photo by Carlo Allegri/Getty Images

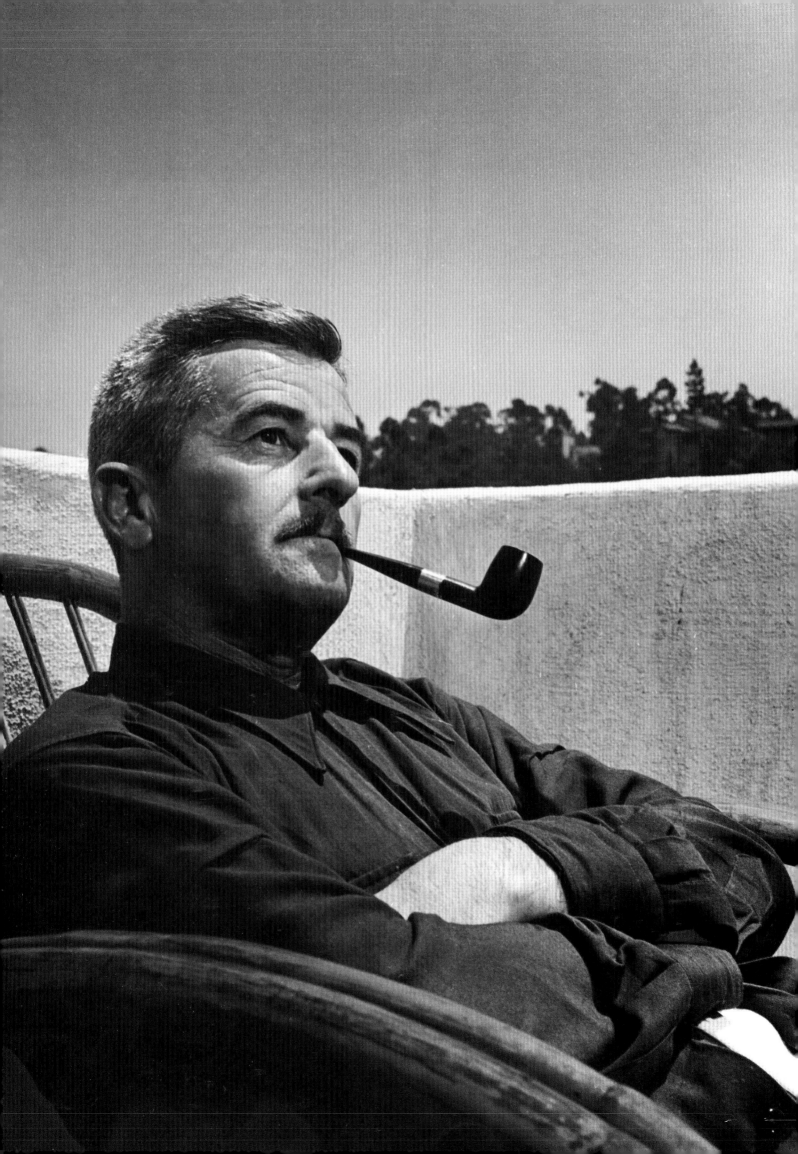

# WILLIAM FAULKNER

'"Oh, Mr. Faulkner, do you write?"
*Clark Gable*
"Yes, I do, Mr. Gable . . . what do you do?"
*William Faulkner*

Before he created his famously fictitious Yoknapatawpha County and gained the status of America's greatest writer, William Faulkner was a University of Mississippi dropout, receiving the lowest grades among his classmates in his sophomore English courses. Nearly fifty years after his death, Faulkner's *The Sound and the Fury*, *As I Lay Dying*, *Light in August*, and *Absalom, Absalom!* are still regarded as the finest works of literature ever written by an American author.

Faulkner was born in New Albany, Mississippi in 1897. When he was four years old, his family moved to nearby Oxford — the place Faulkner called home for the rest of his life. His desire to be a writer began at an early age: his great-grandfather, William Clark Falkner (Faulkner added the "u" to his name as an adult), wrote several "hard-boiled" novels, and at least one of them, *The White Rose of Memphis*, was a commercial success. As a child, Faulkner was reported to say, "I want to be a writer like my great-granddaddy."

Following Faulkner's failed attempt at academia and a brief sojourn in Paris, he went to New Orleans, where he met literary giant Sherwood Anderson. Anderson encouraged Faulkner to write what he knew the most about, namely, North Mississippi. Faulkner returned to Oxford and created Yoknapatawpha County, based on the people and landscapes of Lafayette County, and the town of Jefferson, a literary mirror image of Oxford. Faulkner wrote with a force of pure language on the sentence level never before seen in American literature. Many readers found his books impenetrable, and he was little known to the general reading public until he won the Nobel Prize for Literature in 1949.

William Faulkner died on July 6, 1962 in Byhalia, Mississippi, and he was buried in St. Peter's Cemetery in Oxford, Mississippi.

**Photograph** William Faulkner smoking a pipe on a Hollywood balcony, early 1940s.
Photo by Alfred Eriss/Pix Inc./Time Life Pictures/Getty Images • **Story** by Louis Bourgeois

# TENNESSEE WILLIAMS

**"You have been as brave as anyone I've known . . . ."**

*From Marlon Brando in a letter to Williams*

Tennessee Williams wrote to stay sane. That's how he coped with a smothering mother, a lobotomized sister, and a father who called him Miss Nancy.

Born in 1911 as Thomas Lanier Williams in Columbus, Mississippi, he spent his early childhood in Clarksdale, which inspired a peculiar southern ambiance and names like Cutrer, Wingfield and Blanche in his plays. Though his family moved to St. Louis, Missouri when he was seven, Williams returned to spend summers with his Episcopalian grandfather, the Reverend Dakin, and continued to call Mississippi home.

The St. Louis years proved so volatile, Williams spent a lifetime writing to put them in context. As his creativity developed, so did his name — from Tommy to Tom to Tennessee. In 1945, his semi-autobiographical play, *The Glass Menagerie*, debuted on Broadway and changed the core of American theatre.

His innovative use of poetic realism connected audiences to the internal struggles of characters. Describing Tennessee's writing, John Patrick Shanley said, "He cuts through time and space with a voice as gigantic as the night sky." Williams' plays, including *A Streetcar Named Desire* and *Cat on a Hot Tin Roof*, garnered two Pulitzer Prizes, four New York Drama Critic's Circle Awards, and a Tony Award, among others.

Williams' book, *Memoirs* — which openly examines his homosexuality, substance abuse, and struggle for sanity — provides insight into his work and the condition of those "trapped by circumstance." In 1980, three years before his death, President Carter honored him with the Presidential Medal of Freedom for showing "the truly heroic in life or art is human compassion."

**Photograph** Tennessee Williams at his typewriter. Photo by Alfred Eisenstaedt//Time Life Pictures
**Story** by Kate McCalley Hooper

# B.B. KING

**"All I did was copy B.B. King."**
*Eric Clapton*

As a boy, Riley B. King played guitar on Mississippi Delta street corners for dimes. Sometimes he would play four towns a night. That persistence never diminished. In 1956, B.B. King played a record-breaking 342 concerts.

As reigning "King of the Blues" for more than half a century, King defines the blues for millions.

He has produced more than 50 records, he has won 15 Grammy Awards, and he was an early inductee into the Rock and Roll Hall of Fame.

As a guitarist, his economic, waste-no-note style has influenced Eric Clapton, Jeff Beck, and George Harrison.

The man whom *Rolling Stone* magazine listed as number three of the "100 Greatest Guitarists of All Time" still spends 250 days a year touring. Not bad for an 86-year-old. Long live the King — and his companion Lucille.

**Photograph** of B.B.. King at Club Ebony, Indianola, Mississippi
by Tom Davis

# MORGAN FREEMAN

**"One of the most respected performers in American cinema."**

*Kennedy Center Chairman Stephen A. Schwarzman*

Morgan Freeman starred in his first play in Charleston, Mississippi at the age of nine. Three years later, he won a statewide drama competition in the capital city of Jackson. He's a natural. And he feels perfectly natural in his movie roles — whether he's playing a criminal, a cop, a deity or a dignitary.

His distinctive voice makes him one of the most sought-after narrators in entertainment (his primary competition is fellow Mississippian James Earl Jones). His notable voice-over work includes *March of the Penguins*, *The Shawshank Redemption*, *The CBS Evening News*, and countless advertisements. He won an Academy Award for *Million Dollar Baby* in 2005, and was Oscar-nominated for four other performances. Other awards include a Golden Globe and several Screen Actors Guild Awards.

Freeman brings dignity to his characters — from a prisoner in *The Shawshank Redemption* to a cowboy in *Unforgiven*; from a chauffeur in *Driving Miss Daisy* to an inventor in *Batman Begins*; and from an African-American Major in *Glory* to a trainer in *Million Dollar Baby*. He's an actor's actor. Hollywood stars clamor to play opposite him in films. But Freeman never forgets his Mississippi roots. He is committed to improving the lives of fellow Mississippians through environmental awareness, racial reconciliation, literacy programs, and philanthropic enterprise. He has been granted honorary degrees from Rhodes College and Brown University. And he was recognized with a Lifetime Achievement Award from the Mississippi Institute of Arts and Letters.

Hollywood's choice to play Nelson Mandela, President of the United States, and God, Freeman remembers his youth. And that's his secret. He taps into his past to make characters real.

**Photograph** courtesy of Luxury Equestrian Lifestyle Magazine by Chris Polk/FilmMagic

# JIM HENSON

**"My hope is to leave the world a bit better than when I got here."**
*Jim Henson*

Artist. Visionary. Television pioneer. Mississippi native Jim Henson revolutionized entertainment, education, and culture as creator of some of the world's most memorable characters — including the king of green, Kermit the Frog. And it all started in the tiny town of Leland, Mississippi.

Throughout his youth in the 1930s and 1940s in Leland, Mississippi, Henson didn't show much interest in hunting, fishing, and farming like most Delta boys. Instead, he had an interest in art. His grandmother, an avid painter and needleworker, was supportive of Henson's artistic efforts from the start. She spent tremendous time with her grandson and encouraged him to use his imagination. Little did she know she was kindling a flame that would ignite an entire artistic movement.

When Henson was in fifth grade, his family relocated to Maryland. There, he expanded his interests into the evolving world of television. In 1954, while still in high school, he launched his career by performing with puppets on a Washington, DC Saturday morning program. The following year, as a freshman at the University of Maryland, he was given his own twice-daily, five-minute production, *Sam and Friends*.

While working on that show, Henson joined forces with fellow student and future wife, Jane Nebel, to introduce his unique brand of humor and innovative technical tricks — and Muppets, Inc. was born.

By 1966, Henson had created a family of characters for a ground-breaking children's show called *Sesame Street*. For more than 40 years, Bert and Ernie, Oscar the Grouch, and Big Bird have entertained and educated children across the world.

But Henson didn't stop there. With the success of *Sesame Street*, he saw the opportunity to reach a broader audience. Henson once commented, "The most sophisticated people I know — inside they are all children." Soon, Henson created *The Muppet Show* and introduced Miss Piggy and Fozzie Bear. His characters have since been seen in Hollywood feature films, including six Muppets movies, *The Dark Crystal*, and *Labyrinth*. His expansion to the big screen launched Jim Henson's Creature Shop, which continues to set industry standards in animatronics and performance technology.

**Photograph** Henson posed with muppet mural, circa 1986. Photo by Nancy R. Schiff/Getty Images • **Story** by Julie Cantrell

# JOHN GRISHAM

**"The bestselling author in the world."**
*Guinness Book of World Records*

John Grisham may be the bestselling author in the world, but you wouldn't know it to meet him. He's friendly, reserved, down-to-earth and polite. Over the years Grisham went to work early each morning when his children were young so they would understand the importance of work ethic. He has refused to accept cameo appearances in the films based on his books, and he even took his turns teaching Sunday school.

There are currently more than 250 million John Grisham books in print. The books have been translated into 29 languages. Nine of his novels have been turned into films.

It all started one day at the DeSoto County courthouse when Grisham overheard the harrowing testimony of a twelve-year-old rape victim. He was compelled to write a novel about what would have happened had the girl's father murdered her assailants. Getting up at 5 a.m. every day to get in several hours of writing time before heading off to work, Grisham spent three years on *A Time to Kill* and finished it in 1987. It was rejected by 28 publishers, until a small publisher printed 5,000 copies. Shortly thereafter, the small press filed bankruptcy. Grisham bought the remainder of his books — and sold them from the trunk of his car. That might have put an end to the writing career of many a struggling attorney, but the day after Grisham completed *A Time to Kill*, he began work on another novel — the story of a hotshot young attorney lured to an apparently perfect law firm that was not what it appeared. When he sold the film rights to *The Firm* to Paramount Pictures for $600,000, Grisham suddenly became a hot property among publishers, and book rights were bought by Doubleday. Spending 47 weeks on *The New York Times* bestseller list, *The Firm* became the bestselling novel of 1991.

The successes of *The Pelican Brief*, which hit number one on the *New York Times* bestseller list, and *The Client*, which debuted at number one, confirmed Grisham's reputation as the master of the legal thriller.

When he's not writing, Grisham devotes time to charitable causes, including most recently his Rebuild The Coast Fund, which raised 8.8 million dollars for Gulf Coast relief in the wake of Hurricane Katrina. He also anonymously funds many social, legal, and creative endeavors. And he also keeps up with his greatest passion: baseball. The man who dreamed of being a professional baseball player now serves as the local Little League commissioner. The six ballfields he built on his property have hosted more than 350 kids on 26 Little League teams.

Grisham and his wife Renee split their time between a Victorian home on a farm in Mississippi and a plantation near Charlottesville, Virginia.

**Photograph** of John Grisham delivering keynote address at the Robert C. Khayat Law Center dedication ceremony, Oxford, Mississippi. Photo courtesy of The University of Mississippi

# JERRY RICE

Crawford, Mississippi

**"He *is* the greatest receiver . . . and maybe the greatest football player of all time."**
*Five-time All-Pro safety Darren Sharper*

The odds were stacked against wide receiver Jerry Rice going into the 1985 NFL draft. Sure, Rice's college numbers were impressive: a record-setting 50 career touchdowns, more than 300 catches, and nearly 5,000 yards. But he put up those astronomical stats at tiny, historically black Mississippi Valley State University in Itta Bena, Mississippi.

Although Rice was named to every All-American team and finished ninth overall in Heisman balloting, most NFL scouts considered him untested against the best defensive players and worse, slow, with a below-average 40-yard dash time.

But those hands. The son of a bricklayer from Crawford, Mississippi, Rice's hands were huge, strong, and seemed to pluck passes out of the air. Those hands inspired a San Francisco 49ers scout to convince Coach Bill Walsh to get Rice, even if it meant trading other picks in the draft.

The gamble paid off. Rice and quarterback Joe Montana combined for the most potent scoring machine in NFL history, winning three Super Bowls for the 49ers. Rice is the all-time leader in every statistical category for pro wide receivers, including touchdowns with 208.

Regarded as the best wide receiver in NFL history, Rice was inducted into the Pro Football Hall of Fame in 2010.

**Photograph** by Walter Iooss Jr./Sports Illustrated • **Story** by Ace Atkins
*Ace Atkins' father, Bill Atkins, was the 49ers scout who knew Jerry Rice was something special.*

# BRETT FAVRE

**"He's the best, bar none."**

*Cris Carter, All-Pro Receiver*

The greatest quarterback of all time. A lofty dream for any kid. Especially for a young man from the rough little Mississippi town known as "the Kill" (spelled Kiln).

Favre tripped along the way. In high school, his father (who also coached his team) believed in the running game. Favre averaged about five passes per game. He was offered just one college scholarship (from the University of Southern Mississippi in Hattiesburg). His first year as a pro was not only disappointing — it was embarrassing.

Favre's career turned around when Ron Wolf, general manager of the Green Bay Packers, took a chance on the inexperienced quarterback. Favre led the Packers to seven division championships, as well as a Super Bowl victory in 1997. He was voted the NFL's Most Valuable Player three years in a row. And Favre now holds 24 NFL records, including most career touchdowns, most career passing yards, most career pass completions, most consecutive starts, and most career victories as a starting quarterback.

In 2009, at age 40, he led the Minnesota Vikings to the National Football Conference championship game.

Coaches everywhere hold Favre up as an example for young players. When it comes to work ethic, durability, and love of the game, no one quite compares.

And for those of us who don't work in the profession, Favre offers a different kind of lesson. A lesson in second chances. His first year as a professional player in Atlanta, he threw just four passes — two incompletions and two interceptions.

**Photograph**: Sportsman of the Year, Portrait of Green Bay Packers QB Brett Favre. Photo by Walter Iooss Jr./Sports Illustrated

# LEONTYNE PRICE

**"Voice is what counts,
and voice is what Miss Price has."**
*New York Times Review*

Not many singers have what it takes to transition from being a blue-collar Mississippi girl singing in the church choir to a *prima donna* soprano performing for capacity opera crowds across the world, but that's just what Leontyne Price managed to accomplish.

Born in Laurel, Mississippi in 1927, Price credits her musical talent to her mother, a midwife who sang to Price throughout her childhood and enrolled her in piano lessons at the age of five. Her mother also took nine-year-old Price to see American opera singer Marian Anderson perform in Jackson.

It was that performance that set Price on the path to opera. Not the typical life course for an African-American southern girl in those days, but thanks to her supportive parents, Price won a full-tuition scholarship to the prestigious Juilliard School of Music in 1948 and launched one of the most phenomenal musical careers of all time.

With a voice described by critics as "dusky and rich in its lower tones, perfectly even in its transitions from one register to another, and flawlessly pure and velvety at the top," Price made a tremendous impact on the opera world. Standing ovations to sold-out audiences became the norm for Price as she performed in top venues across the globe, but one of the highlights of her career occurred when she received a record-setting 42-minute ovation for her portrayal of Leonora in Verdi's *Il Trovatore* at New York City's Metropolitan Opera.

Price will always be recognized as one of the greatest musical performers of the 20th century, but her faithful fans may never have heard her voice at all, if she hadn't once sat in her stroller in Laurel, Mississippi and listened to her mother sing.

**Photograph** of Leontyne Price singing in her farewell performance, "Aida" at the Metropolitan Opera House, New York City.
Photo by Sara Krulwich/New York Times Co. • **Story** by Julie Cantrell

# JIMMY BUFFETT

**"Go down to the local bar, to the waterfront where the fish are cleaned, and listen to the local people. That's where you get your information."**
*Jimmy Buffett*

Margaritaville. Parrothead. Landshark. These are just a few of the words coined by singer, songwriter, author, and businessman Jimmy Buffett, who has successfully shared the Gulf Coast culture with the world.

Born to a family of "gypsies and sailors," Buffett has always lived a life in motion. He's known as an island hopper with a microphone in one hand and a margarita in the other, but his Mississippi roots run deep.

A Pascagoula native, Buffett describes his Gulf Coast homeland as paradise: "I was born and raised on the shores of the northern Gulf of Mexico. To me it is the northern edge of the Caribbean. The night sky and constellations above Pascagoula look pretty much the same as those above Martinique."

With that kind of coastal playground as a child, Buffett developed a strong connection to the water and the wind. By the time he attended the University of Southern Mississippi in Hattiesburg, he was already making a big impression with his unique lyrics and pirate personality.

With a strong grassroots following across the South, Buffett recorded and toured continually. Loyal fans shared the albums with friends and helped build momentum. Then came the release of his chart-topping single "Margaritaville" and his first platinum record. While the record industry still had no accurate label for Buffett, it was clear that he had created the ultimate good-time music, a laugh-at-life celebration in song.

Buffett has released more than 40 albums, most with gold, platinum, and multi-platinum status. He has won a Country Music Association Award and two Academy of Country Music Awards, has received two Grammy nominations, and has been inducted into the Nashville Songwriters Hall of Fame. He has found success with his Margaritaville restaurants, stores, and Internet radio station Radio Margaritaville; has ventured into the world of movie production; and has become a bestselling author. He is one of only nine authors in the history of the *New York Times* bestseller list to have reached number one on both fiction and non-fiction lists. He also has his aviation license and continues to explore the seas and the skies as the "son of a son of a sailor."

**Photograph** by Frank Capri/Getty Images • **Story** by Julie Cantrell

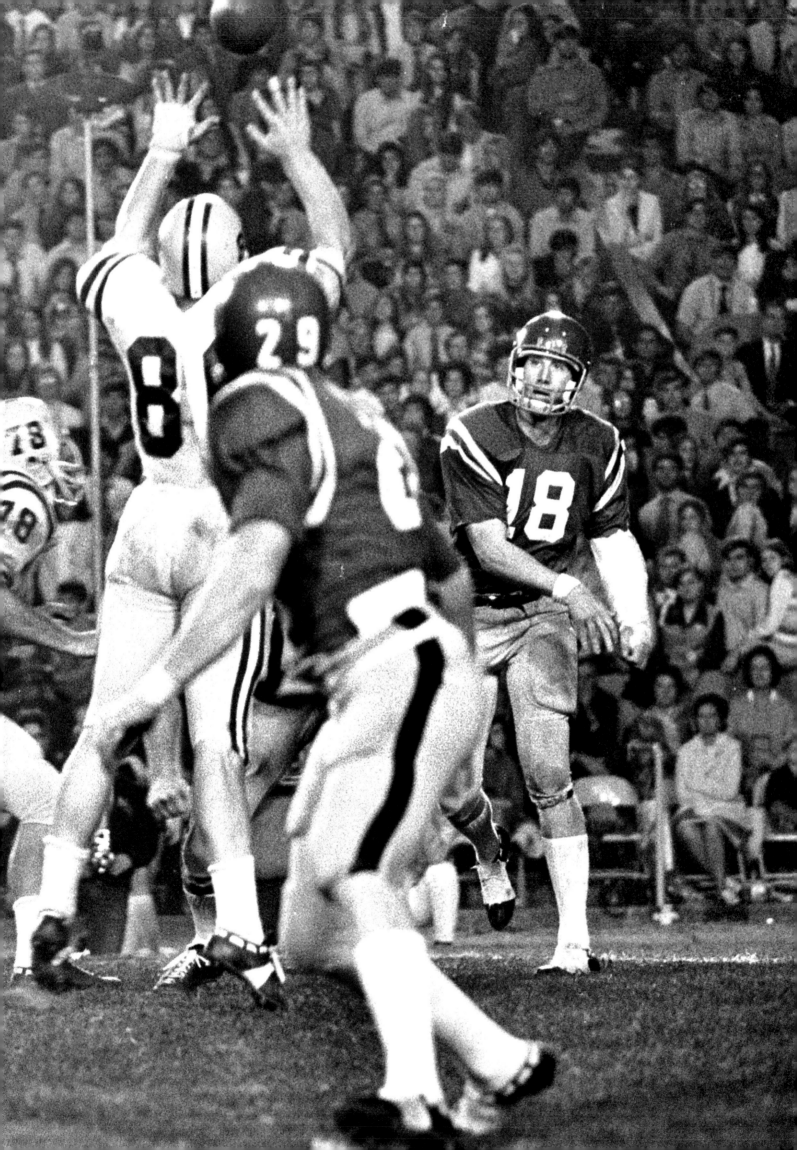

# ARCHIE MANNING

**"Archie became legend larger than life."**
*John Grisham*

Every boy growing up in Mississippi in the late 1960s or early 1970s wanted to be Archie Manning. The soft-spoken quarterback who inspired a song — *The Ballad of Archie Who* — was one of the most exciting college quarterbacks to ever play the game. Paul "Bear" Bryant said, "He's the finest college quarterback I've ever seen play." Archie's scrambles, weaving back and forth across the football field, left fans breathless. If not for a broken arm his senior year, he probably would have won the Heisman Trophy.

As a professional, Archie was a shining star for the New Orleans Saints (a team often described as "dreadful"). His record as a pro was 35-101-3, the worst in NFL history among quarterbacks with at least 100 starts. Despite being surrounded by less-than-stellar teammates, in 1972, Archie led the NFL in pass attempts and completions (and led the NFC in passing yards). That year the Saints' record was 2-11-1. In 1978, Archie was the NFC player of the year. The Saints' record: 7-9. It could be said that his greatest contributions to professional football are his sons — Peyton and Eli.

# WALTER PAYTON

**"Walter Payton was the best football player I've ever seen, and probably one of the best people I've ever met."**
*Mike Ditka*

In the highly competitive world of the NFL, it takes guts to have a nickname like "Sweetness." But that's what friends called one of the finest running backs of all time, Walter Payton. Born in Columbia, Mississippi in 1954, Payton made as much of an impression off the field as he did on the turf. His strong character might be grounded in some good ol' Mississippi dirt.

In hopes of keeping her sons out of trouble, Payton's mother ordered a pile of topsoil each summer. While other kids ran the streets, her boys stayed busy building ramps and camps across their yard. When they weren't digging, the Payton boys hiked and fished — and played every sport.

For Payton, that meant three years of football at the all-black John Jefferson High School before his senior year brought big changes. Columbia High was integrated, and Payton found himself one of the first black students to don a Columbia High uniform. He made the transition seamlessly, and Payton was on his way to becoming one of the most influential American athletes of all time.

In college, Payton excelled in athletics and academics. He studied education for the hearing impaired and finished fourth for the Heisman Trophy — no small accomplishment for a player from little-known Jackson State University. He was a first-team All-American and the Black College Player of the Year in 1973 and 1974.

The pros came knocking and he signed with the Chicago Bears (he missed only one game throughout his 13-season career). As a pro, Payton won the NFL's Most Valuable Player Award twice and retired with two NFL rushing records. In 2000, the NFL Man of the Year Award was renamed the Walter Payton NFL Man of the Year Award to recognize Payton's spirit.

Always looking for a way to help others, Payton said, "If you can catch children at a young age, you can really change a life." Maybe that's what his mother was thinking each summer when she ordered that load of Mississippi dirt.

**Photograph** by Jonathan Daniel/Getty Images • **Story** by Julie Cantrell

# EUDORA WELTY

**"I am a writer who came of a sheltered life.
A sheltered life can be a daring life as well.
For all serious daring starts from within."**
*Eudora Welty*

The Pulitzer Prize, the Presidential Medal of Freedom, and the National Medal of Arts are just a few of the honors that have been bestowed upon Mississippi author and photographer Eudora Welty. But her proudest accomplishment may be that she succeeded at living a simple southern life.

Born in Jackson in 1909, Welty experienced no particular hardships during her formative years and admits she came from a happy Mississippi family who read books aloud to one another in the evenings. Perhaps that's why she was known for having an open mind, a charming sense of humor and a compassionate soul.

Those traits were expanded during the 1930s, when Welty returned from college to land a publicity job with the Works Progress Administration (WPA). It was a powerful period for the nation, with some of the worst effects of the Great Depression felt in rural Mississippi, where Welty was assigned. The people she met and places she explored proved ideal for story development, as she put her thoughts to paper and penned one literary wonder after another. With character-driven plots in charged southern settings, Welty quickly became recognized as one of America's most influential fiction writers.

Welty shined a different kind of light on the human condition than one might expect. One thing that set her apart from other esteemed writers of her day was her ability to focus on the tolerance, generosity, and goodness of humanity. As she honed her craft, Welty celebrated the power of love, rather than the failure of it; she examined, with great admiration and reflection, the varied stages of life.

With more than 20 published books, Welty's long, happy life ended in July, 2001. But for legions of fans the world over, she will always be remembered as the heart of the American South.

**Photograph** courtesy Lemuria Bookstore, Jackson, Mississippi
**Story** by Julie Cantrell

# JAMES EARL JONES

**"I think the extent to which I have any balance at all, any mental balance, is because of being a farm kid and being raised in those isolated rural areas."**

*James Earl Jones*

"This is CNN." That famous TV line represents America's most powerful voice. Now think of Darth Vader from the *Star Wars* films and the respected King Mufasa from *The Lion King*. These are just a few of the characters who have become cultural icons thanks to legendary actor James Earl Jones.

Born in 1931 in the tiny township of Arkabutla, Mississippi, Jones was raised by his maternal grandparents. While he credits his grandparents for having a positive influence on his life, Jones admits his parents' abandonment affected him deeply. "No matter how old the character I play," he said, "those deep childhood memories, those furies, will come out."

Jones' grandparents understood the importance of home and gave him the perfect setting to heal. He spent his early childhood hunting, fishing, and farming in rural Mississippi, where he was able to feel free.

By the age of five, the adoption became official and Jones relocated with his grandparents to Michigan. But leaving the South proved difficult, as Jones developed a severe stutter that made him reluctant to speak.

Thankfully, his grandparents weren't the only ones to see his potential. A dedicated high school teacher encouraged him to enter speaking contests. This helped him learn to speak fluently again and did wonders for his self-esteem.

A stellar student, Jones earned a degree in theater from the University of Michigan, where he attended on full scholarship. Then, a postgraduation move to New York City brought Jones to the forefront of the theater circuit.

He quickly landed a number of small roles. Critics took notice, more acclaimed stage work followed, and numerous awards paved the way to Jones' 1968 Tony Award and a 1970 Oscar nomination for his performances in both the Broadway and film versions of *The Great White Hope*.

Jones has appeared in countless memorable roles and has been recognized with dozens of honors, including a National Medal of Arts Award, a Screen Actors Guild Lifetime Achievement Award, and several Emmy and Golden Globe Awards and nominations.

**Photograph** of Jones with a copy of Howard Sackler's play "The Great White Hope."
Photo by Bernard Gotfryd/Getty Images • **Story** by Julie Cantrell

# MOVIES, TV & STAGE

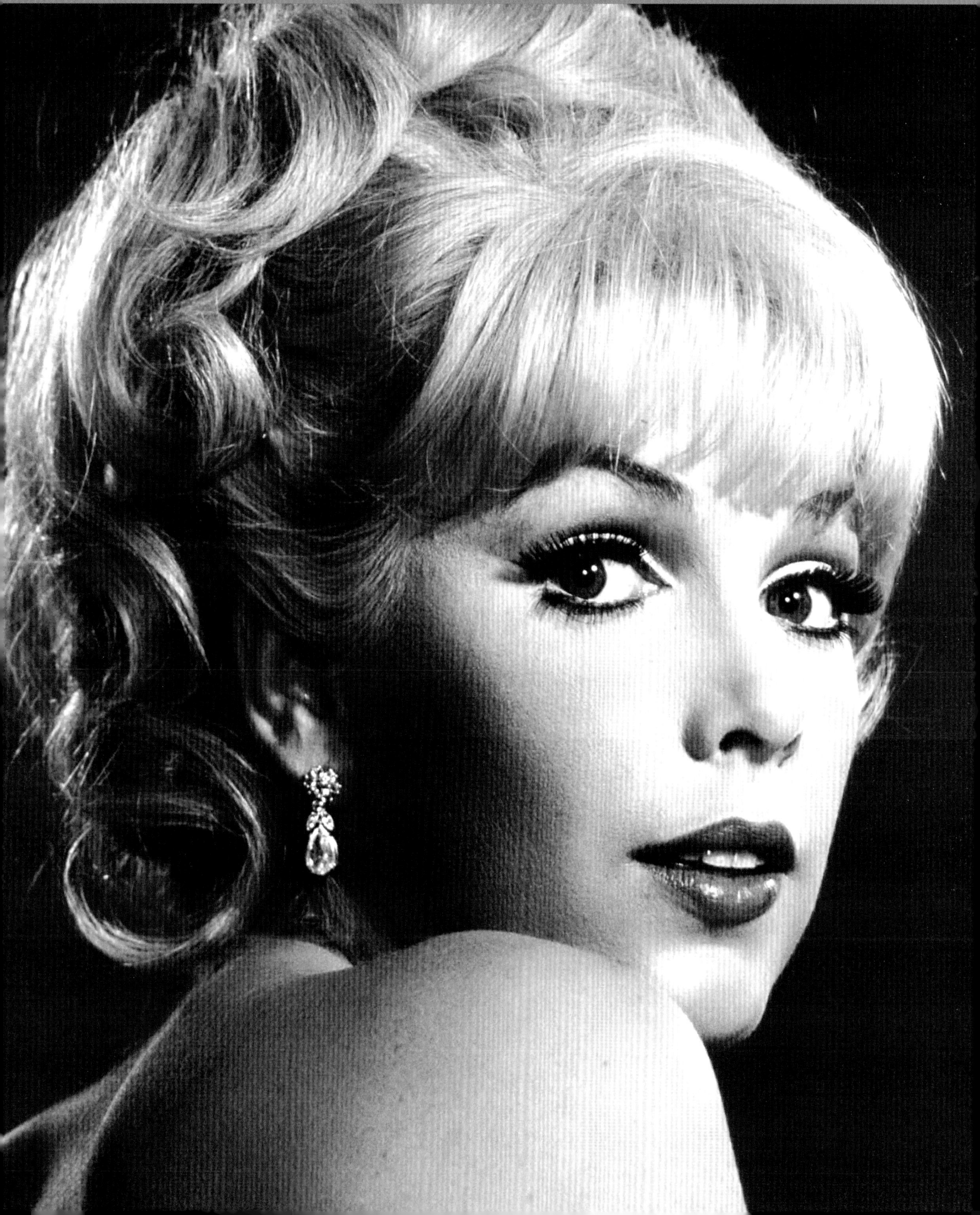

# SELA WARD

**"So much of my life has been about returning home and longing for home, wanting my children to know about my roots."**

*Sela Ward*

Homesick. That's how actor Sela Ward described herself in 2002 when she gave the same title to her memoir and returned home to her birthplace, Meridian.

Ward was born in July 1956 to a homemaker and an electrical engineer. That simple southern life gave Ward the stability and confidence she needed to step into the competitive world of acting.

She may have been a small town girl, but she had plenty of strong women as role models, and could hold her own in the big city. Modeling work landed her a few commercials, including a coveted TV spot for Maybelline. At that time, Ward joked that Maybelline 24-hour Fresh Lash Mascara sent her to 18 voice lessons because she still had such a southern accent.

Accent or not, Ward's commercial appearances led to dramatic roles throughout the 1980s and eventually brought her the chance to portray the colorful Teddy Reed on the award-winning drama series *Sisters*. Thanks in large part to Ward's conflicted character, the show developed a broad following and enjoyed a successful six-season run.

Her role on *Sisters* led to a 1994 Emmy for Outstanding Lead Actress in a Drama Series, as well as nominations for both a Golden Globe and Screen Actors Guild Award. She also won an Emmy and a Golden Globe for her work on another long-running series, *Once & Again*.

Ward has starred in motion pictures and television features with co-stars including Burt Reynolds, Tom Hanks, Harrison Ford, and Kelsey Grammer.

Ward has reduced her time on stage and screen to focus on her role as a mother. She and her husband have built a family home in Meridian and developed Hope Village, an emergency shelter for children awaiting placement in foster homes. Located on 30 acres in Meridian, the shelter helps more than 200 children each year and allows Ward to give something back to the hometown that gave her a strong and healthy start.

**Photograph** at *The Day After Tomorrow* New York Premiere. Photo by Dimitrios Kambouris/WireImage • **Story** by Julie Cantrell

# PARKER POSEY

**"The Queen of Indies."**

*Hollywood Reporter*

**"I wouldn't say I was a queen.
Maybe a little elf."**

*Parker Posey*

Parker Posey, named for 1950s model Suzy Parker, was born in Baltimore in 1968, but moved to Laurel, Mississippi when she was 12 with her parents and twin brother. Her father owned Posey Chevrolet in Laurel, and her mother worked as a chef and culinary instructor for the Viking Range Corporation in Greenwood. Parker moved to New York to study acting, but dropped out a few weeks short of graduation to accept a role on the soap opera *As the World Turns*.

Her first major film role came shortly thereafter in the cult classic *Dazed and Confused*. A critically praised performance in the film — audiences love her sardonic wit and slightly quirky beauty — led to more roles in indie films;  so many, in fact, that Posey is often referred to as "The Queen of Indies."  Posey is a remarkably flexible actress, however, and seems to transition easily between blockbusters such as *You've Got Mail*, in which she played Tom Hanks' book-editor girlfriend, to indies such as the campy canine *Best in Show*, in which Posey's character — not the dog she owned — clearly stole the show.

**Photograph** by Corey Sipkin/NY Daily News Archive • **Story** by Beth Ann Fennelly

# TATE TAYLOR

WRITER, DIRECTOR, ACTOR

Tate Taylor once stole a fetal swine from his Jackson Prep biology class so he could shoot a realistic horror film about a girl giving birth to a pig. That kind of dedication paid off. Two decades later he found himself at DreamWorks Studios, talking film with Steven Spielberg, sharing his vision for the cinematic version of *The Help*. Because Taylor and Kathryn Stockett were childhood friends, the up-and-coming director was able to begin work on adapting *The Help* into a major motion picture before it even hit bookstores. Taylor, by the way, has not only directed, but has starred in several films and television shows, including HBO's *Six Feet Under* and the critically acclaimed film *Winter's Bone*.

*The Help* opened to $25.5 million at the box office in its first weekend. Peter Debruge, of *Variety*, wrote, "[*The Help*] serves as an enlightening and deeply affecting exercise in empathy for those who've never considered what life must have been like for African-Americans living with inequality a full century after the Emancipation Proclamation called an end to slavery."

**Photograph**: Tate Taylor (director of *The Help*) and Octavia Spencer (star of *The Help*). Photo by Matt McClain, *The Washington Post*.

# DAVID SHEFFIELD

SCRIPTWRITER

In the late 1970s, while working for an advertising agency in Biloxi, Mississippi, David Sheffield mailed unsolicited comedy sketches to *Saturday Night Live*. His work was so impressive the producers hired him as a full-time writer in 1980. As a new hire, Sheffield chose to work with the newest, youngest *Saturday Night Live* cast member — a 19-year-old kid named Eddie Murphy. Sheffield and Murphy partnered to write some of the show's most memorable characters: Buckwheat, Gumby, and Mr. Robinson (Sheffield also wrote the lyrics for "Hot Tub" — the James Brown spoof). By 1983, Sheffield was head writer and supervising producer at *Saturday Night Live*.

In 1984, Sheffield and his writing partner Barry Blaustein moved to Los Angeles to pursue screenwriting full-time. Their films — *Coming to America*, *The Nutty Professor*, *The Nutty Professor II*, and *Boomerang* — have grossed over a billion dollars.

**Photograph** of Barry Blaustein (left) and David Sheffield (right) on the set of Saturday Night Live. Photo courtesy Cynthia Walker.

# JOEY LAUREN ADAMS

ACTOR, WRITER, DIRECTOR

**"A quietly powerful film."**

New York Observer *on Adams'* Come Early Morning

Joey Lauren Adams, star of *Chasing Amy* and *Mallrats*, lives in Oxford, Mississippi. An accomplished actress — in both independent and big-budget films — Adams received a Golden Globe nomination for her part in the movie *Chasing Amy*. Other notable film appearances include roles in *Big Daddy* and *The Break-Up*. Her most recent television role is a kind-hearted barmaid in *United States of Tara* who falls for "Buck," one of the male personas of the lead female character who suffers from a multiple personality disorder.

Adams' debut as a writer and director came in 2006 with the film *Come Early Morning* (an official Sundance Film Festival selection). Of her relocation to Oxford, she noted, "Someone said if you stay in Oxford long enough, everyone will come here. . . ."

**Photograph** Joey Lauren Adams at the premiere of *Trucker*, Tribeca Film Festival. Photo by Bennett Raglin/WireImage

# DANA ANDREWS

ACTOR

Born on a farm in Covington County, Dana Andrews was one of 13 children born to a Mississippi minister. In 1931, he hitchhiked to California and took a series of menial jobs while trying to make it big in Hollywood. His humble southern roots kept him grounded as he drove a bus, dug ditches, picked oranges, stocked shelves and pumped gas. His average-Joe manners might be what interested the gas station owner to invest in Andrews' talent, putting up the money to send him to opera training and enrolling him in the Pasadena Community Playhouse. His talents were noticed immediately on stage and screen. With nearly 70 films to his credit — including *Kit Carson*, *Laura*, *Tobacco Road*, and *The Battle of the Bulge* — Andrews became one of the biggest stars throughout the 1940s. He is best remembered for his role as a lynching victim in the 1943 masterpiece, *The Ox-Bow Incident*. He also served as president of the Screen Actors Guild.

**Photograph** Dana Andrews in *The Right Hand Man* on Playhouse 90. Photo by CBS

# LAWRENCE GORDON

PRODUCER

If you're an action film fan, you've seen one of Mississippi Delta native Lawrence Gordon's movies. He produced *48 Hours*, *Predator*, *Die Hard*, *Field of Dreams*, *Point Break*, and *G.I. Jane*, among 20 others. After graduating from Tulane University, he was hired by Aaron Spelling. Spelling recognized Gordon's knack for picking winners. Soon, Spelling and Gordon were co-producing television and film projects.

From 1984-1986, the boy who grew up in Belzoni served as president of 20th Century Fox.

**Photograph** Producer Lawrence Gordon speaks at the 22nd Annual Producers Guild Awards. Photo by Kevin Winter

# GARY GRUBBS

ACTOR

One of the most successful character actors of modern times is living an inconspicuous life with his wife and two children in the university town of Hattiesburg, Mississippi. Born in Amory, and a supportive alumnus of the University of Southern Mississippi where he played for the Golden Eagles football team, Gary Grubbs has stayed true to his roots despite a steady line-up of acting gigs across the country. He portrayed attorney Al Oser in Oliver Stone's controversial film *JFK*, and landed roles in major productions such as *Silkwood* and *The Astronaut's Wife*. He also had recurring roles on several TV hit series, including *Growing Pains*, *Will & Grace*, *Touched by an Angel*, *The X-Files*, *E.R.*, *The O.C.*, and most recently, *Treme* on HBO.

Grubbs co-starred in *Game-Time: Tackling the Past* with Beau Bridges. Upcoming roles in television and film include *No One Lives*, *Alabama Moon*, *Hell and Mr. Fudge*, *Weather Wars*, *Shadow People*, *Carjacked* and the TNT movie, *Ricochet*. He also starred in a pilot for a series based on Bull Durham.

With more than 200 roles to his credit, Grubbs may be one of the hardest working actors in Hollywood today.

# BRUNSON GREEN

PRODUCER

Brunson Green, a native of Jackson, Mississippi, is the president of L.A. film production company Harbinger Pictures. Green's most recent and lucrative project was *The Help*, which he produced alongside director and fellow Mississippi native Tate Taylor. Kathryn Stockett, author of the book, *The Help*, said of the duo, "I can't think of a better team to bring *The Help* to the screen. We grew up within a one-mile radius of each other in Jackson, Mississippi." One of the most sought-after film projects in recent years, the $100 million production was released in theaters in August 2011. Brunson has also produced several other films, including *Pretty Ugly People* and *Chicken Party*.

**Photograph:** Producer Brunson Green with author Kathryn Stockett and actor Octavia Spencer. Photo by Eric Charbonneau

# MARY DONNELLY HASKELL

SINGER, ACTOR

**"I love how there is no exact definition of, or limitation to, how we 'make a joyful noise unto the Lord.' The important thing is that we make one!"**

*Mary Haskell*

Mary Donnelly Haskell has always had a passion for singing. The Oxford resident has released three CDs, the most recent, *Just in Time For Christmas*. Haskell attended the University of Mississippi, where she met her husband, Sam Haskell. In 1977, she competed as Miss Mississippi in the Miss America Pageant. Though she loved performing on stage, and performed in such places as The White House, The Kennedy Center, and onboard the Presidential Yacht Sequoia, she switched to TV and film after becoming a mother, with notable recurring and guest starring roles on *Sisters*, *Touched By An Angel*, *The Martin Short Show*, *Diagnosis Murder*, and *7th Heaven*. She has starred in over 20 TV movies including the ratings hits *Once Upon A Christmas* and *Twice Upon A Christmas* for Hallmark and ABC Family. Mary and her husband Sam Haskell (see facing page) have two children, Sam IV and Mary Lane.

# SAM HASKELL

HOLLYWOOD POWERHOUSE

**"Sam Haskell is an anomaly in Hollywood."**

*Leslie Moonves, President of CBS*

Raised in Amory, Mississippi, Sam Haskell graduated from Amory High School and the University of Mississippi. He was the long-time Worldwide Head of Television for The William Morris Agency in Beverly Hills and helped nurture and package dozens of hit TV shows including *The Cosby Show*, *Fresh Prince of Bel Air*, *Who Wants to be a Millionaire?*, *Everybody Loves Raymond*, and *Lost*. His client list included Bill Cosby, Dolly Parton, Ray Romano, George Clooney, Whoopi Goldberg and Kathie Lee Gifford (pictured below). Haskell recently released his bestselling autobiography *Promises I Made My Mother*, in which he highlights his mother's lessons of integrity and honesty. His commitment to those values led to his unlikely success in a sometimes less-than-civil Hollywood culture. Sam lives in Oxford, Mississippi, with his wife, former Miss Mississippi and recording artist, Mary Donnelly Haskell. Sam and Mary have two children, Sam IV of Los Angeles, and Mary Lane of New York.

# KATE JACKSON

ACTOR

Kate Jackson attended the University of Mississippi before heading off to acting school in New York. The film and television actress has snagged four Emmy Award nominations. Jackson is best known for her role as "Sabrina" in the series *Charlie's Angels*. She also starred in *Scarecrow & Mrs. King*. She is now a spokeswoman for the American Heart Association.

**Photograph** by ABC Photo Archives

# DIANE LADD

ACTOR

Since her birth in Meridian, Mississippi, Diane Ladd has starred in many successful films and television shows — most notably *Alice Doesn't Live Here Anymore* (1974), for which she received an Academy Award Best Supporting Actress nomination. She was nominated for this same honor two more times during her career, for her performances in *Wild at Heart* (1990) and *Rambling Rose* (1991). Ladd also had roles in *Mississippi Burning* and Joey Lauren Adams' film *Come Early Morning*.

She is the mother of Laura Dern and the second cousin of another notable Mississippian, playwright Tennessee Williams.

**Photograph:** Diane Ladd touches her star after she received her Hollywood Walk of Fame. Photo Ark Ralston/AF

# JOHN MAXWELL

ACTOR, PLAYWRIGHT

Master playwright and actor John Maxwell grew up just outside of Pickens, Mississippi — "Just past the *Resume Speed* sign," Maxwell quips. But that's where he discovered drama. When Maxwell was five years old, he performed in local talent shows, a time he recalls as "one of the most exciting theater experiences of my life."

While most actors relocate to Hollywood or New York, Maxwell became one of the few Mississippi thespians to build a lasting, full-time career all based from home. He is best known for his award-winning one-man show, *Oh, Mr. Faulkner, Do You Write?* (the world premiere was held at Jackson's New Stage Theatre in 1981). Maxwell has performed the play internationally to rave reviews for more than two decades. In his spare time, he writes plays, teaches creative writing, leads acting workshops, and performs monologues throughout the South.

Maxwell now teaches at Belhaven University.

**Photograph** from the play, *Oh, Mr. Faulkner, Do You Write?*

# MARY ANN MOBLEY

ACTOR

Most women would consider wearing the crown as Miss America enough of an achievement for one lifetime. When Mary Ann Mobley was crowned in 1959, however, she was just beginning to make her mark on the world. Mobley became one of the few Miss Americas to see significant success as an actor and singer. She appeared opposite Elvis Presley in two films and received a 1965 Golden Globe followed by a long string of high-profile acting roles on both stage and screen. A Mississippi girl at heart, Mobley has been vocal about her devout Christian faith and is an avid philanthropist. "I grew up in the church," she once said, "and I feel very strongly about it."

**Photograph** of Mary Ann Mobley as a guest star in the "Ship of Ghouls" episode of *The Love Boat*.
Photo by ABC Photo Archives

# GERALD MCRANEY

ACTOR

Television and film actor Gerald McRaney grew up in Collins, Mississippi and attended Ole Miss. He has appeared in many television shows throughout the years, but he is best known for his starring roles in *Simon & Simon* and *Major Dad*. McRaney is an avid supporter of veterans and visited troops during Operation Desert Storm. He landed a recurring role in *Designing Women*, and it was there that he met his wife, actress Delta Burke.

**Photograph** of Gerald McRaney and his wife, Delta Burke (whose character Suzanne Sugarbaker on *Designing Women* was a Pi Phi at Ole Miss).
Photo by Time & Life Pictures

# STELLA STEVENS

ACTOR

**"Stella Stevens was born to be in the movies. . .and to drive men crazy!"**
*Director Henry Hathaway*

Stella Stevens (real name Estelle Caro Eggleston) grew up in Hot Coffee, Mississippi. She played opposite Elvis Presley in *Girls! Girls! Girls!* Other films include Sam Peckinpah's *The Ballad of Cable Hogue*, *The Nutty Professor*, and *The Poseidon Adventure* (as Ernest Borgnine's prostitute wife, Linda Rogo). She has appeared in three dozen major motion pictures.

**Photograph** by Photoshot

# RAY WALSTON

ACTOR

Perhaps most famously known for his role as "Uncle Martian" in the popular television series *My Favorite Martian*, Ray Walston grew up poor in Laurel, Mississippi. He had a long career in Hollywood, mostly playing small character roles. He appeared in dozens of television shows including *Mission Impossible*, *The Six Million Dollar Man*, *Little House on the Prairie*, *The Incredible Hulk*, and as "Boothby" in *Star Trek: The Next Generation*.

Fans of coming-of-age films will remember Walston as Mr. Hand, the antagonistic history teacher who foiled Sean Penn's "Spicoli" in *Fast Times at Ridgemont High*.

**Photograph** of Ray Walston from the "A Double for Danger" episode of *The Mod Squad*. Photo by ABC Photo Archives

# BENJI

ACTOR

When this little girl was picked up by animal control in Pass Christian, she was running loose with a collie. After seven days in the animal shelter, no one claimed her. That's when Robin Bush, a Gulfport native, stepped in and pulled her from an untimely demise. Robin placed her with a family while she underwent heartworm treatment.

Then, a nationwide casting call for the "new" Benji was issued. Bush made sure her new friend made the auditions. The former homeless 3-year-old beat out 400 others. The rest is history.

She still lives with Benji creator and producer Joe Camp and his family in Tennessee.

**Photograph** courtesy Mulberry Square Productions

# JULIE KAYE FANTON

AWARD-WINNING SET DECORATOR

Julie Kaye Fanton has worked as a set decorator in film and television since 1980. A native of Oxford, she graduated from Ole Miss with a degree in Theatre Arts in 1979. She won an Emmy Award for *Rogers and Hamerstein's Cinderella* in 1998 and was nominated for *Sabrina the Teenage Witch* in 2003. She also recieved a nomination for an award from the Art Directors Guild for *My Name is Earl* in 2008. Along with her professional work Julie is CEO of the nonprofit "Uganda Development Initiative," which builds schools and supports education and commerce in southwestern Uganda.

# JOHN DYE

ACTOR

Best known for his character of Andrew the "Angel of Death" on the TV series *Touched by an Angel*, John Dye began acting in high school productions in Tupelo. While attending the University of Memphis, he landed his first major role in *Making the Grade* with Judd Nelson, which led to his first leading role in *Campus Man* in 1987. He re-teamed with Nelson on the TV mini-series *Billionaire Boys Club* and then in 1989 he starred with James Earl Jones and Eric Roberts in the martial-arts film *Best of the Best*. While originally cast as a recurring character, he became a regular cast member on *Touched by an Angel*. The show ran for nine seasons. Dye passed away at his home in San Francisco, CA in January 2011.

# RUTH FORD

ACTOR

**"One of the nicest people in Hollywood is William Faulkner, who I had known in Mississippi when I was getting my Masters Degree in Philosophy at the University there."**

*Ruth Ford*

uth Ford followed her brother, bohemian artist Charles Henri Ford, to New York City, where she became a model (for Mann Ray and Cecil Beaton), an actress and a muse to artists. Orson Welles assisted her in landing contracts with Columbia Pictures and Warner Bros. and she acted in dozens of B-movies in Hollywood. Greater acting success came to her onstage in more than a dozen Broadway productions. In 1959 Ms. Ford starred in the only play written by William Faulkner, *Requiem for a Nun*. The role of Temple Drake in the play was written expressly for her and she played opposite her husband Zachary Scott, whom she married in 1950. By her death at age 98 in 2009, her apartment in the famed Dakota Hotel had become a salon extraordinaire for writers, artists and musicians.

"My life has been too exciting, too wonderful," she said, "to let anything else, and that includes acting, come first."

**Photograph** Actress Ruth Ford in a scene from the stage play *Any Wednesday*. Photo by Ray Fisher/Time Life Pictures

# TOM LESTER

ACTOR, INSPIRATIONAL SPEAKER

In 1965, a young Tom Lester auditioned for a tiny role in a television sitcom originally titled *Country Cousins*. More than 400 other young actors vied for the spot, but Lester was cast as Eb Dawson, the hired hand, in the show eventually re-titled *Green Acres*.

Lester's character turned out to be so popular that Eb appeared in virtually every episode. With his signature "Golly, Mr. Douglas," his ability to translate the snorts of Arnold the pig, and his habit of addressing the Douglases as "Mom and Dad," Lester's Eb became a 1960s cultural icon.

After *Green Acres'* run, Lester, a Laurel native, moved into feature films and guest appearances on *Little House on the Prairie* and *Marcus Welby, M.D.* Lester's most recent project is a short film — *Huntin' Buddies* — costarring Mel Tillis and Tim Conway.

Lester lives on a farm outside Laurel, Mississippi. He spends his time as an inspirational and motivational speaker. He has appeared with Billy Graham, Paul Harvey and Paul "Bear" Bryant.

# M.C. GAINEY

ACTOR

**"With a face like this, there aren't a lot of lawyers or priest roles coming my way."**

*M.C. Gainey*

A veteran character actor who embraces the role of villain, M.C. Gainey worked as an undertaker's apprentice before enrolling in the American Conservatory Theater in San Francisco. Gainey's first role was in the Steve Martin film *Pennies from Heaven*.

Gainey has appeared in more than 50 movies including *Breakdown*, *Con Air*, *The Mighty Ducks*, *Terminator 3* and *Sideways* (he was the naked guy running down the street).

On his role as Swamp Thing in *Con Air*, Gainey noted, "Not that the role merits careful examination . . . [but] I'm not really such a bad guy. I'm just a guy who likes to fly."

Gainey has also guest starred in more than 40 television series, including *Designing Women*, *Cheers*, *CSI* and *The X Files*. Most recently he appeared on 20+ episodes of *Lost* as Tom Friendly, an influential member of "The Others."

**Photograph** by J. Vespa/WireImage

# ROBERT EARL JONES

ACTOR, BOXER

Born in Senatobia in 1904, Robert Earl Jones was a grade-school dropout, a sharecropper, and a prizefighter (he was a sparring partner of Joe Louis). He allegedly, and often, lied about his age in order to promote his boxing career. Eventually, Jones made his way to New York City where he started acting.

His first play, in 1945, was *The Hasty Heart*, followed by *Set My People Free* (1948). Other plays included *Infidel Caesar* (1962) and *Death of a Salesman* (1975).

Jones appeared in more than twenty films, including *The Cotton Club* and *The Sting* (as Luther Coleman, an aging grifter). He also had recurring roles in the television series' *Kojak* and *Lou Grant*.

One of his last stage roles, a 1991 production of *Mule Bone*, was co-produced by Langston Hughes and Zora Neale Hurston.

Jones' career, though successful, didn't compare to his son's, James Earl Jones. The elder Jones passed away in 2006, purportedly, at the age of 102.

**Photograph** Robert Earl Jones (right) walks along Bleeker Street (with his son James Earl Jones) on their way to attend the Obie Awards.
Photo by Fred W. McDarrah

# HATTIE MAE WINSTON

ACTOR

Born in Lexington and raised in Greenville, Hattie Mae Winston realized her talent for acting and singing early on. After moving to New York, she got her acting start as a replacement performer in Broadway's 1969 *Hair* production and landed her first starring role in *The Tap Dance Kid* in 1983. She has also appeared in films and on TV, with roles in *Homefront* and *True Crime*. Always collecting scripts and screenplays written by African-Americans, Winston donated the Hattie Winston African-American Scripts and Screenplays Collection to the University of Louisville in Kentucky.

**Photograph** by Steve Grayson/WireImage

# ANTHONY HERRERA

ACTOR

Wiggins native Anthony Herrera is best known, loved, and hated, for his role as the evil James Stenbeck on the soap opera *As the World Turns*. From 1980 until 2010, he reprised the role, suffering many "final deaths" and "surprise returns." In 1984 he directed the documentary *Mississippi Delta Blues* and in 1987 he adapted and directed the TV movie version of Eudora Welty's *The Wide Net*. In New York, he co-founded The Poetry Theatre, an online theater featuring actors reading their favorite poems. He marked his longtime battle with cancer in his book *The Cancer War* and testified before Congress in support of stem cell research. Herrera passed away in Buenos Aires in June 2011.

# RITCHIE MONTGOMERY
ACTOR

**W**hat a character. Natchez native Ritchie Montgomery's career as an actor has spanned over thirty years and spawned nearly one hundred characters, including recurring roles on the TV series *Clunkers* and *The Dukes of Hazzard*. His film career includes roles in *The Green Lantern*, *The Help*, *Catch Me if You Can*, *Monster's Ball* and the voice of Reggie in the animated feature *The Princess and the Frog*.

# CAT CORA

TV CHEF

The only woman on *Iron Chef America*, Cat Cora began developing her plans to open a restaurant as early as age 15. Raised in Jackson, Cora grew up eating meals of Southern food combined with her family's traditional Greek recipes; this combination was the inspiration for her first cookbook, *Cat Cora's Kitchen*, which was published in 2004. Since then, she has published two more cookbooks, appeared on several cooking shows, and worked with Michelle Obama's Chefs Move to Schools campaign in an effort to improve nutrition in schools.

# MART CROWLEY

SCRIPTWRITER

After heading to Hollywood in 1957, Vicksburg native Mart Crowley found work as an assistant to Natalie Wood, which gave him time to write his play *The Boys in the Band*. The play opened off-Broadway in 1968 to rave reviews and ran for 1001 performances. The film adaptation enjoyed similar success and is thought to be among the first gay-themed films in motion-picture history. He won the Los Angeles Drama Critics Circle award nomination for his autobiographical play *A Breeze from the Gulf*. *The Men from the Boys* was Crowley's sequel to *The Boys in the Band*.

**Photograph:** Actor Griffin Dunne (left) and scriptwriter Mart Crowley attend the *Making the Boys* New York premiere.
Photo by John Lamparski/WireImage

# BEAH RICHARDS
### ACTOR

A native of Vicksburg, Mississippi, Beah Richards' career took off in 1955 when, at age 35, she played an 84-year-old grandmother in the off-Broadway show *Take a Giant Step*. She appeared in the original Broadway productions of *The Miracle Worker* and *A Raisin in the Sun*, and was nominated for a Tony Award when she played Sister Margaret in James Baldwin's *The Amen Corner* in 1965. She also appeared in films such as *Beloved* and *In the Heat of the Night*, and was nominated for a Best Supporting Actress Academy Award when she played Sidney Poitier's mother in *Guess Who's Coming to Dinner* (though she was only seven years older than him). Beah Richards passed away in her hometown of Vicksburg in 2000.

**Photograph** of Beah Richards in Roots: The Next Generation. Photo by ABC Photo Archives

# JERRY CLOWER
COMEDIAN, AUTHOR

Always one to make folks laugh, Liberty, Mississippi native Jerry Clower graduated from Mississippi State University with a degree in agriculture and landed a job as director of field services for the Mississippi Chemical Company. While there, he charmed coworkers and clients with stories about the rural South. He once said, "I don't tell funny stories, I tell stories funny." His colleagues encouraged him to make a comedic recording, and his first album sold more than 8,000 copies without being advertised. Bigger labels came knocking, and soon *The Coon Hunt* album went platinum. Clower became a top name in comedy, releasing more than 32 recordings. His greatest hits album sold over 500,000 copies.

**Photograph** courtesy Michael Ochs Archives

# JIM DEES

Jim Dees spent nearly a decade working at the infamous, now defunct Hoka Cinema. Ron Shapiro, proprietor of the Hoka, first recognized Dees' gift for writing and decided to publish an alternative paper — *Off Times* — primarily to showcase Dees' talents (his weekly column was titled "Lifestyles of the Poor and Obscure"). Dees has been writing ever since.

Now, he is host of the wildly popular Thacker Mountain Radio Show. His quick wit and quirky observations keep the live audience in stitches. During a recent show, when the musical guests revealed they were 19- and 20-year-olds, Dees announced, "I have restraining orders older than that."

Dees edited the anthology *They Write Among Us: New Stories and Essays from the Best of Oxford Writers*. A collection of his best newspaper columns were published in 2008 under the title *Lies and Other Truths: Rants, Raves, Low-Lifes and Highballs* (including essays like "My Dog Can Mix Drinks" and "Pulp Fishin'").

He lives, writes, and drinks in Taylor, Mississippi.

**Photograph** by Bethany Cooper

# LYNDA LEE MEAD SHEA

Lynda Lee Mead was crowned Miss America in 1960. The Miss America who passed along the crown was another Mississippian, Mary Ann Mobley. After her reign as Miss America, she married the prominent Memphis physician, Dr. John Shea. They have three children.

Shea, a graduate of the Parsons School of Design, is the owner of French Country Antiques and Shea Interiors, a successful interior design firm. Shea has served on the Board of the Assisi Foundation of Memphis for many years. Shea is a member of the University of Mississippi Hall of Fame and has endowed scholarships at the university.

**Photograph** Miss America Lynda Lee Mead is honored with a parade in her home town, Natchez, Mississippi (1960)
Photo by Bates Littlehales/National Geographic

SPORTS

# ELI MANNING

**"Eli leads by example."**

*NY Giants coach Tom Coughlin*

In Super Bowl XLII, Eli Manning orchestrated a last-minute drive to lead the New York Giants to victory over the heavily-favored New England Patriots. It solidified his place as a superstar in the National Football League.

The youngest son of NFL great Archie Manning, Eli was a first-round draft choice; he holds just about every quarterback record at Ole Miss, and his list of national awards includes the Conerly Trophy, the Maxwell Award, SEC Player of the Year, and Super Bowl XLII Most Valuable Player.

During the off-season, the laid-back, unflappable Manning (his teammates call him "Easy") lives with his wife in Oxford, Mississippi.

**Photograph** Eli Manning after the Giants defeated the New England Patriots 17-14 in Super Bowl XLII.
Photo by Andy Lyons/Getty Images

# STEVE MCNAIR

**"I want people to say when No. 9 was out on the field, he did everything humanly possible to win a ball game."**

*Steve McNair*

Steve McNair was the most prolific offensive player in NCAA history. By the end of his career at Alcorn State University, McNair had racked up more than 16,000 yards of offense (a record that still stands). As a quarterback for 13 seasons in the NFL, McNair was a three-time Pro Bowler, as well as the NFL's Most Valuable Player in 2003. He retired in 2007 as the Tennessee Titans' all-time leading passer, accumulating 31,304 yards during his career.

**Photograph** Steve McNair looks to throw the ball during an NFL football game against the Baltimore Ravens in 1999.
Photo by Mitchell Layto

# RALPH BOSTON

**"Being the first to cross the finish line makes you a winner in only one phase of life.
It's what you do after you cross the line that really counts."**

*Ralph Boston*

Laurel native Ralph Boston was the first man on Earth to long jump over 27 feet. He was considered an average jumper until the 1960 Olympics when he shattered Jesse Owens' 25-year-old record and won the Gold Medal. The ultimate gentleman on the track, Boston continued to compete in subsequent Olympic games, each time losing to a competitor to whom he had offered advice. One of those competitors was teammate Bob Beamon who, in 1969, after taking Boston's recommendation to back up a few inches on his start, broke the previous record by more than two feet (a feat *Sports Illustrated* ranked in the top five greatest sports moments of the 20th century). Boston is a member of the National Track and Field Hall of Fame and the Olympic Hall of Fame.

**Photograph** Mississippian Ralph Boston breaks the world record for long jump in Rome in 1960.
Photo by John G. Zimmerman/*Sports Illustrated*

# DIZZY DEAN

**"Play to win, but play fair, in sports and in life."**

*Dizzy Dean*

As pitcher for the St. Louis Cardinals, the Chicago Cubs, and the St. Louis Browns, Jay Hanna "Dizzy" Dean is remembered as one of America's most colorful pro baseball players. Known as a bragger with an over-the-top personality, Dean's spunk provided a healthy dose of flavor for the Great Depression-era fans and led him into a post-play career as a national sports broadcaster. Dean had no children, but he dreamed that one day every young person would have the opportunity to play ball. Throughout his career, he set many pitching records and was elected to the baseball Hall of Fame; but Dean's legacy may be his dedication to helping kids succeed in sports. Dean and his wife retired in her Mississippi hometown, Bond, where he is buried.

In one game against the Chicago White Sox, Dean struck out 11 batters. The White Sox manager told his players, "He's making you boys look dizzy." The name stuck.

**Photograph** by *Sporting News*

# DAVE "BOO" FERRISS

**"Stick to the books."**

*Boo Ferriss to author John Grisham, during try-outs when*
*Grisham failed in his attempts to hit a college-level curve ball*

Shaw native Boo Ferriss was the first baseball player to receive a full scholarship to Mississippi State. He went on to pitch for the Boston Red Sox. He pitched a two-hitter in his first game with the Red Sox in 1945 — and would go on to set the American League record for scoreless innings to start a career (a record that stood for 63 years). In 1946, Ferriss won 13 consecutive games at Fenway Park (also still a major league record). Ferriss was pitching coach for the Red Sox for four years, and then accepted the position of head coach of the baseball team at Delta State University. The nickname? As a child he couldn't say the word "brother."

**Photograph** courtesy Mississippi Sports Hall of Fame & Museum

# WILL CLARK

**"Will Clark ranks number 26 among the top 50 all-time at first base."**

*The Baseball Pages*

In high school, Will Clark was called "Will the Thrill" because of his natural talents on the baseball field. After leading Mississippi State to the College World Series (and playing on the 1984 U.S. Olympic team), Clark made an immediate impact in professional baseball. His first swing in the major leagues (against Nolan Ryan) went for a home run. Clark was voted the starting first baseman for the National League All-Star team every season from 1988 through 1992. In 1990, Clark signed a $15 million, four-year contract, making him the highest-paid player in baseball at the time. He is a member of the College Baseball Hall of Fame, as well as the Mississippi Sports Hall of Fame.

**Photograph** by Rich Pilling

# LANCE ALWORTH

**"A player comes along once in a lifetime who alone is worth the price of admission. Lance Alworth was that player!"**

*Charley Hennigan, NFL receiver*

Lance Alworth epitomized the glamorous, crowd-pleasing approach to football the AFL San Diego Chargers exhibited in the early years of the league. Alworth's patented leaping catches and blazing after-the-catch runs are legendary (his nickname was Bambi). Statistics are often misleading, but in Alworth's case, they are not.

In eleven pro seasons, he caught 542 passes for 10,266 yards (an 18.94-yard average) and scored 85 touchdowns. During his nine seasons with the Chargers, the graceful receiver averaged more than 50 catches and 1,000 yards per season. Alworth was the first AFL star to be inducted into the Pro Football Hall of Fame.

In 1958, the Brookhaven High School star — who was headed to Ole Miss after graduation — married before leaving for college. Ole Miss coach Johnny Vaught had a strict policy against offering scholarships to married men, so Alworth enrolled at Arkansas where he was an All-American. It may have been the worst decision of Vaught's career.

**Photograph** by Russ Reed/*Sporting News*

# HENRY ARMSTRONG

**"The second greatest fighter of the last 80 years."**

*Ring Magazine*

The 5-foot, 5-inch Armstrong won the World Featherweight Championship in 1937. In 1938, he added the World Welterweight Title. Later in the year, he won the World Lightweight belt. The man known as "Homicide Hank" is the only boxer to ever hold three world titles simultaneously. And this was accomplished during a time when there were only eight weight classes. His streak of 27 straight knockouts is one of the longest in history. The Columbus native's purses totaled nearly $1 million, but most of the money was gone by the time he was 32 (at one point, singer Al Jolson purchased his contract). After retirement, Armstrong was ordained as a Baptist minister.

**Photograph** of Henry Armstrong (circa 1938). Photo by Popperfoto

# CHARLIE CONERLY

**"I've never coached a football player who had more courage."**
*Vince Lombardi*

A natural on the field, All-American "Chunkin' Charlie" astonished Rebel football fans during his time at Ole Miss. The Clarksdale native set three NCAA records for the Rebels' SEC Championship team before becoming Rookie of the Year as quarterback for the New York Giants (he threw 22 touchdowns his rookie season — a record that lasted 50 years until it was eclipsed by Peyton Manning's 23). He was later named NFL Player of the Year and enjoyed a successful 14-year NFL run. Toward the end of Conerly's career, a newly hired Giants coach was stuggling with gaining the respect of the other players. He went to Conerly for advice on how to relate to professional ball players. Conerly's words must have been memorable. That coach was Vince Lombardi.

Conerly also was hired to be America's favorite cowboy – the Marlboro Man. Today, The Conerly Trophy is awarded each year to the best college football player in Mississippi.

**Photograph** by Robert Riger, Getty Images Sport

# L.C. GREENWOOD

L.C. Greenwood, the Pittsburgh Steelers' reckless pass rusher, is widely regarded as one of professional football's greatest defensive linemen. Standing 6-feet, 6-inches, weighing in at 250 pounds, and wearing his signature gold-colored cleats, Greenwood helped form the famous "Steel Curtain" defensive unit alongside the great "Mean Joe Green." A Canton native, Greenwood, who played in six Pro Bowls, helped the Pittsburgh Steelers win four Super Bowl victories.

Greenwood was nicknamed "Hollywood Bags" because he claimed to keep his bags packed to be ready to leave for Hollywood at a moment's notice.

**Photograph** L.C. Greenwood during Super Bowl XIV. Photo by Bill Smith

# RAY GUY

**"He's the first punter you could look at and say, 'He won games.'"**

*Joe Horrigan, Pro Football Hall of Fame historian*

The *Sporting News* called him "the finest punter in the history of the world." John Madden said "Ray Guy was the only draft choice our coaches and scouts agreed on unanimously." And Oakland Raiders owner Al Davis said of Ray Guy, "He's the best *ever* to play his position."

All this fuss over a punter? You bet. Guy, an All-American at USM in 1972, kicked a 93-yard punt against Ole Miss (still an SEC record). He was a seven-time All-Pro for the Oakland Raiders, he kicked 619 times without a single block, he never had a punt returned for a touchdown, and he was the only punter selected for the NFL's 75th Anniversary All-Time Team. Known for his power, Guy inspired the "hang time" statistic (one team actually had the ball pulled and tested for helium), and he was the first punter to hit the Louisiana Superdome's video screen.

**Photograph** courtesy Getty Images Sports

# PATRICK WILLIS

**"I've coached two of the greatest linebackers — one that has already proven to be one of the greatest and one who will prove to be."**

*NFL Hall of Famer Mike Singletary, referring to Ray Lewis and Patrick Willis*

During Patrick Willis' senior season at Ole Miss, he was awarded the Butkus Award and the Jack Lambert Award as the nation's top linebacker. A year later as a member of the 49ers, Willis led the NFL in tackles, earned First Team All-Pro and Pro Bowl honors while being named the 2007 NFL Defensive Rookie of the Year. Willis has earned Pro Bowl and All-Pro honors all four years he has played in the NFL. He is the only player to receive the Butkus Award for best linebacker as a collegian and a professional.

Willis is considered by many as the best inside linebacker in professional football.

**Photograph** courtesy Getty Sports

# ARCHIE MOORE

**"Number four among the 100 greatest punchers of all time."**

Ring Magazine

Ranked as the number five all-time Light Heavyweight, Benoit native Archie Moore was the Light Heavyweight belt-holder for 11 years. He actively fought for 27 years (one of the longest careers on record) and was the only boxer to fight against two of the most feared Heavyweight champions — Rocky Marciano and Muhammad Ali. His 131 career knockouts is still a record. An avid supporter of youth programs, "Ageless Archie" spent most of his retirement volunteering to help America's youth and was elected to the Boxing Hall of Fame.

**Photograph** Heavyweight champion Rocky Marciano (right) falls to his knees after Archie Moore's short right connects to Marciano's jaw. Photo by Charles Hoff/*New York Daily News* Archive

# JENNIFER GILLOM

An Ole Miss All-American, Olympic Gold Medalist, and 1985 USA Basketball Athlete of the Year, Jennifer Gillom was a pioneer player in the Women's National Basketball Association and is now revered as one of the league's top coaches. Gillom grew up in Abbeville, Mississippi with six brothers and three sisters. Her sister, Peggy, is also a basketball coach. The sisters were honored when the University of Mississippi renamed an athletic facility the Gillom Sports Complex. Gillom has traveled extensively with international teams, speaks both Italian and Greek, and holds several amateur and professional records. In 2009, she was inducted into the Women's Basketball Hall of Fame.

**Photograph** by Juan Ocampo/NBAE

# COOL PAPA BELL

**"Once he hit a line drive right past my ear. I turned around and saw the ball hit his butt sliding into second."**

*Satchel Paige*

Some baseball historians have argued that James Thomas "Cool Papa" Bell was the fastest man to ever play professional baseball. Bell stole 175 bases in a single season and once rounded the bases in an unofficial twelve seconds (the official record is 13.3 seconds). He was a star in the Negro Leagues from 1922-1950. His lifetime batting average was .419.

His nickname came from an extraordinary calm in front of baseball crowds. In 1974, the Starkville native was inducted into the Baseball Hall of Fame.

**Photograph** courtesy Mississippi Sports Hall of Fame & Museum

# LEM BARNEY

Whether he was returning punts, kickoffs, or interceptions, Gulfport native Lem Barney was the most feared return man in the NFL for more than a decade. A second-round draft choice out of Jackson State, Barney won Defensive Rookie of the Year honors in 1967. He played in seven Pro Bowls and was inducted into the Pro Football Hall of Fame in 1992 — only the fifth cornerback to be inducted.

**Photograph** Detroit Lions Hall of Fame cornerback Lem Barney in a 1969 game at Tiger Stadium. Photo by Tony Tomsic/Getty Images

# JAKE GIBBS

**"In the long, distinguished history of Ole Miss athletics,
we have never had a better athlete than Jake Gibbs."**
*Robert Khayat*

*Sports Illustrated* ranked Jake Gibbs as the eighth best college quarterback of the modern era. An All-American quarterback at Ole Miss, Gibbs led the Rebels to three post-season victories. The Grenada native was the SEC Player of the Year in 1960, as well as the Sugar Bowl's Most Outstanding Player.

Gibbs was also an All-American baseball player at Ole Miss. He turned down several professional football offers. Instead, he played for ten years with the New York Yankees. In 1971, he retired from professional baseball. He was the head coach of the Ole Miss baseball team for 19 seasons.

**Photograph** Jake Gibbs, catcher for the New York Yankees, poses for a portrait in Yankee Stadium.
Photo by: Kidwiler Collection/Diamond Images

# HUGH GREEN

**"Hugh Green is the most productive player at his position I have ever seen in college."**

*John McKay, Tampa Bay Buccaneers Coach*

In 1980, Natchez native Hugh Green won the Walter Camp Award, the Maxwell Award, and the Lombardi Award. *The Sporting News* named him Player of the Year. Green finished second in the Heisman Trophy balloting (the highest finish *ever* for a Mississippian — and the highest a defensive player had ever finished ). A first-round draft choice, Green played in the NFL for ten seasons. Twice he played in the Pro Bowl.

**Photograph** by George Gojkovich, Getty Images Sport

# BAILEY HOWELL

A consensus All-American at Mississippi State, Bailey Howell led the nation in field goal percentage his sophomore year. He still holds scoring and rebound records at MSU. Generally regarded as the greatest basketball player in Mississippi history, Howell was a six-time NBA All-Star. He was elected to the Naismith Memorial Basketball Hall of Fame in 1997.

**Photograph** Bailey Howell grabs a rebound during a game Boston, Massachusetts
Photo by Rogers Photo Archive

# BRUISER KINARD

One of Mississippi's earliest football greats, Frank "Bruiser" Kinard, played college ball at Ole Miss. A Pelahatchie native, it is rumored Kinard, an all-around athlete, once put a kick-off deep in the end zone and single-handedly tackled the returner before he reached the goal line. In 1936, Kinard was selected as an All-American — the first ever for Ole Miss. He spent nine years in the pros and was the first Mississippian enshrined in the Pro Football Hall of Fame.

**Photograph** Frank "Bruiser" Kinard at the Ole Miss stadium (circa 1930)
Photo by Mississippi/Collegiate Image

# D.D. LEWIS

**"The best linebacker in the country."**
*Paul "Bear" Bryant*

Dwight Douglas Lewis was a first-team All-American linebacker his senior year at Mississippi State University. He was also selected as SEC Defensive Player of the Year. Lauded as one of the best college linebackers of all time, Lewis spent 14 seasons with the Dallas Cowboys. He is one of only eight NFL players to participate in five Super Bowls.

**Photograph** Dallas Cowboy linebacker D.D. Lewis (left) and quarterback Roger Staubach (right). Photo by Focus on Sport/Getty

# DEUCE MCALLISTER

**"Deuce McAllister has always embodied the spirit of the New Orleans Saints and the city of New Orleans."**

*Sean Payton, New Orleans Saints coach*

As a college football player, Deuce McAllister shattered records at The University of Mississippi. He is the only player in Ole Miss history to record three straight seasons with more than 1000 all-purpose yards. As a beloved New Orleans Saint, McAllister twice played in the Pro Bowl. He holds the franchise record for rushing and touchdowns. He was made honorary captain of the 2009 squad that won Super Bowl XLIV. The Lena native retired from football in 2010.

**Photograph** by Rob Tringali/Sportschrome

# MARY MILLS

Born in Laurel, Mississippi, Mary Mills was always a natural on the golf course. She won the Mississippi State Amateur Championship at the age of 14 — and defended that title for eight consecutive years. She was the number one golfer for four years at Millsaps College (on the men's team). Her first year on the professional tour, she won Rookie of the Year honors. The following year she won the USGA Women's Open. Mills won the LPGA Championship twice in her career. She now lives in Florida where she teaches golf and designs courses.

**Photograph** courtesy Mississippi Sports Hall of Fame & Museum

# JOHNNY VAUGHT

**"Year in and year out, the University of Mississippi plays some of the finest football
in the nation. The reason: Coach Johnny Vaught."**

Time *magazine, 1960*

One of the most revered college coaches of all time, Johnny Vaught led Ole Miss to six SEC titles, and his 1959, 1960, and 1962 teams shared at least one national title. Under Vaught's leadership the Rebels earned 14 consecutive bowl appearances (a record at the time) and only two coaches had a winning record against Vaught — Bear Bryant (4-3-1) and Robert Neyland (3-2).

**Photograph** courtesy Mississippi Sports Hall of Fame & Museum

# MARGARET WADE

**"Margaret Wade methodically assembled a dynasty at Delta State that remains unrivaled in women's basketball."**

*Naismith Memorial Basketball Hall of Fame*

Margaret Wade led the Delta State women's basketball team to three consecutive national championships. The McCool native's record during the championship years was 93-4 (including a 51-game win streak). Wade was the first woman inducted into the Naismith Memorial Basketball Hall of Fame. The NCAA Woman Player of the Year trophy bears her name.

**Photograph** Margaret Wade with 1976 Delta State team. Photo by James Drake/Sports Illustrated

# SAMMY WINDER

**"Winder was never a flashy running back, but his self-described 'tough, grinding-it-out' style of running was consistent, reliable and a great complement to John Elway."**

*The Denver Post*

Sammy Winder—the 1980 NCAA scoring champion at the University of Southern Mississippi — spent eight seasons with the Denver Broncos, leading the team to three Super Bowls. A two-time All-Pro selection, Winder scored 48 touchdowns during his career. After each score, he performed a now-famous celebration dance he called "the Mississippi Mud Walk." During the 1987 season, the Madison native was the leading scorer in the AFC. He appeared on the cover of *Sports Illustrated*.

**Photograph** by John Kelly/Getty Images

# KRIS MANGUM

A college All-American tight end at The University of Mississippi, Mangum graduated with a B.S. in Public Administration. In 1996, he was drafted by the Carolina Panthers — where he played for ten years — and he ranks fifth in all-time receiving for the team. In 2004, he helped lead the Panthers to Super Bowl XXXVIII. After a brief stint coaching at The University of Southern Mississippi, Mangum settled in Petal, Mississippi, where he serves as Vice-President of Magnolia State Bank. He and his wife, Mary Ellen, have four children.

Mangum's father and brother also played in the NFL.

**Photograph** by Sporting News

# JOHN STROUD

John Stroud left his home of New Albany, Mississippi to attend the University of Mississippi and play basketball as an Ole Miss Rebel. Stroud led the SEC in scoring in 1979 and 1980. He is Ole Miss' all-time leading scorer with 2,328 career points (third-most in SEC history). In 1980, he was drafted by the Houston Rockets. A power forward, he played in one NBA season and then played a year in Spain. After several coaching jobs throughout the south, Stroud settled back in his hometown as the coach of the New Albany High School girls' basketball team in 2005. In 2008, he was selected to the Ole Miss All Century Team and inducted into the Mississippi Sports Hall of Fame in 2009.

**Photograph** courtesy the University of Mississippi

# PAUL ELIAS

With a 42-year career in bass fishing, Paul Elias has won six tournaments, including the 1982 Bassmaster Classic at the Alabama River. In 2008, at Falcon Lake in Texas, he established the all-time winning weight record for a five-bass-limit tournament: 132 pounds, 8 ounces. He is considered an expert and innovator of deep cranking, with his own technique creation, kneel n' reel.

# GENE HICKERSON

Gene Hickerson, who was an outstanding fullback in high school, was moved to the tackle position at Ole Miss. He was regarded as one of the best, if not the finest, linemen in the Southeastern Conference at the end of his collegiate career.

Hickerson was drafted by the Cleveland Browns. Initially, he was simply a messenger back (running play to and from the sideline). But, soon he was moved to first string guard, blocking for some of the finest running backs in NFL history.

Prior to Hickerson joining the Browns, there had been just seven runners in the entire history of the NFL to reach 1,000 yards rushing in a season. With Hickerson paving the way, the Browns featured a 1,000-yard rusher in every season but one during his first ten pro seasons. Furthermore, Cleveland featured the NFL's leading ground gainer in seven of those seasons. Hickerson's contributions to those records were recognized when he was named to the NFL's All-Decade Team of the 1960s.

**Photograph** by Tim Culek/Getty Images

# WESLEY WALLS

Wesley Walls is some kind of versatile. He played quarterback in high school . . . until switching to full back his senior year. At Ole Miss, Walls actually played defensive end for three years, but became a linebacker in his senior year. In addition, he played tight end. In a rare move under today's football system, Walls started both positions in a game against Memphis State University. Ultimately, he ended up playing tight end (though he was still utilized on third-down situations as a pass rusher) The Batesville native earned All-American honors as a senior at Ole Miss.

Walls' professional career started off slowly, but as a Carolina Panther, Walls finally broke out as a player. He made the Pro Bowl five times between 1996 and 2001, only missing it during the 2000 season due to injuries that kept him out for 8 games. While at Carolina, he was also the back-up punter.

Upon his retirement, Walls was considered one of the premier tight ends in the game.

**Photograph** Al Bello /Allsport

# WILLYE WHITE

Willye White, one of the most accomplished athletes from Mississippi, was born in Money, Mississippi in 1939. Beginning in her sophomore year of high school, Willye was the first American track and field athlete to compete in five Olympics, from 1956 to 1972. She won the silver medal in the long jump at the 1956 Olympics in Melbourne, Australia. She was only 16 years old at the time. This was the first time that an American woman had ever medalled in that Olympic event. She won a second silver medal at the 1964 Olympic games in Tokyo, this time for a 400-meter relay. In 1981, Willye was inducted into the USA Track & Field's Hall of Fame — one of 11 hall of fame inductions. In 1999, she was named one of the 100 greatest female athletes of the 20th century by *Sports Illustrated*. Willye White died on February 6, 2007.

**Photograph** Willye White at the 1964 Summer Olympics. Photo by Takeo Tanuma/Sports Illustrated

# DEVIN BRITTON

Brandon native Devin Britton won the NCAA Men's Singles Tennis Championship when he was 18 years old — the youngest person ever to win the title (he broke the record held by John McEnroe). After competing as a freshman at Ole Miss, Britton turned pro.

In one of Britton's first professional matches, he drew the world's number one player, Roger Federer. Britton lost the match, but broke Federer's serve twice (a rare feat for any player).

Britton's unusual serve and volley game has garnered great attention on the professional circuit. At 19, he's already a world-class player — and many tennis experts believe Britton has what it takes to go all the way to number one.

**Photograph** Devin Britton serves to Roger Federer during the 2009 U.S. Open. Photo by Matthew Stockman

# MICHAEL OHER

With the blockbuster film *The Blind Side* breaking box office records, many Americans assume they know Michael Oher's story. But many don't realize how much more there is to Michael Oher. He's smart. And not just in the IQ department. He's emotionally intelligent. When people ask about the film depicting his life, he shrugs his massive shoulders and calmly adds, "People can't believe everything they read or hear."

In fact, Oher has written his own version of his rise from poverty. His publisher, William Shinker, said, "Millions of people think they know Michael Oher's story, but they really don't. He gave only two interviews for the book and none for the movie. This is the first time he has been able to tell his story in his own words with details that only he knows, and to offer his point of view on how anyone, no matter their background and upbringing, can achieve a better life."

America will continue to watch the soft-spoken Oher dominate the line for the Baltimore Ravens on Sundays, but there is much more to his life than just football.

**Photograph** by George Gojkovich/Getty Images

# JACK CRISTIL

**"You can wrap this one in maroon and white, my friends!"**

*Jack Cristil*

The voice of Mississippi State men's basketball and football, Jack Cristil began radio-announcing for the Bulldogs in 1953. Named Mississippi Broadcaster of the Year a total of 21 times, Cristil was inducted into the Mississippi Sports Hall of Fame in 1991. In his 58-year career, he called 636 football games and 1,538 basketball games.

Cristil announced his retirement in February of 2011.

**Photograph** courtesy The Mississippi Sports Hall of Fame and Museum

# STEVE SMITH

In his 17th year as head coach of Baylor University's baseball team, Gulfport native Steve Smith has led the program to new heights. Under his leadership, the team had the most successful 10-year run in the school history. He led the 2005 Baylor squad to the College World Series. In 2005, Smith served as head coach of the USA Baseball National Team, and was president of the American Baseball Coaches Association in 2008.

He was inducted into the Baylor Athletics Hall of Fame in 2006.

**Photograph** courtesy Baylor University

# TONY DEES

Gulfport native Tony Dees won the silver medal in the high hurdles at the 1992 Summer Olympics in Barcelona. He then finished third at the 1993 World Indoor Championships, eighth at the 1993 World Championships, third again at the 1997 World Indoor Championships and fourth at the 1999 World Championships.

Dees was inducted into the Ole Miss track hall of fame in 2004.

**Photograph** Tony Dees jumps over a hurdle during the US Olympic Trials in New Orleans, Louisana. Photo by Tim de FriscoAllsport

# KENT HULL

At Mississippi State, Greenwood native Kent Hull earned four football letters as the Bulldogs' center from 1979-1982 before going on to star in the NFL. During Hull's eleven year career in Buffalo, he played in 121 straight games. The Bills enjoyed eight winning seasons and won four consecutive AFC titles. Named to the Pro Bowl three times, Hull was also one of the team's captains for his final seven years.

Most notably, he played for Buffalo during their record four straight Super Bowl appearances from 1991-1994.

Hull was selected to the Greater Buffalo Sports Hall of Fame in 1997, inducted into the Mississippi State University Sports Hall of Fame in 2000, received the Ralph C. Wilson Distinguished Service Award in 2001, was selected to the Mississippi Sports Hall of Fame in 2002 and was the 19th inductee to the Wall of Fame at Ralph Wilson Stadium in Buffalo in 2002.

**Photograph** Kent Hull blocks for Jim Kelly in Super Bowl XXVII. Photo by Al Messerschmidt/NFL Photos

MUSIC

# 3 DOORS DOWN

**"Crackles with energy and crowd-pleasing choruses."**
*Entertainment Weekly on* The Better Life

3 Doors Down's first big single "Kryptonite" propelled them into the national spotlight. Their debut album, *The Better Life*, went platinum six times. They recorded their first single at Lincoln Recording in Pascagoula, Mississippi (which led to their signing with Universal Records) and they now perform as many as 300 concerts a year worldwide. The group founded The Better Life Foundation, which aided the Mississippi Gulf Coast in the wake of Hurricane Katrina.

**Photograph** by Rick Diamond/WireImage

# FAITH HILL

**"Faith Hill is the diva for people who don't like divas."**

*Los Angeles Times*

Country music sensation Faith Hill was born Audrey Faith Perry in Star, Mississippi, and attended Hinds Community College for a short time before moving to Nashville to pursue her musical career. The contralto singer has sold more than 40 million records and topped the country charts repeatedly, with hits like "Mississippi Girl." Hill was also extraordinarily successful in her crossover to the pop genre, after which she won five Grammy Awards, performed at the Academy Awards, and sang the national anthem at the Super Bowl. She is married to country singer Tim McGraw, and they have three daughters.

**Photograph** by M. Caulfield/WireImage

# JERRY LEE LEWIS

**"The best raw performer in the history of rock and roll music."**
*Roy Orbison*

Jerry Lee Lewis — The Killer — is best known for his high velocity rock anthems "Great Balls of Fire" and "Whole Lotta Shakin' Goin' On." At least 14 of his albums have reached number one in the U.S. charts alone. One of the fathers of rock and roll, *Rolling Stone* magazine ranked him number 24 on their list of 100 Greatest Recording Artists of All Time. The performer, whose antics like kicking the piano bench and setting fire to a Steinway are infamous, now lives on a farm in Nesbit, Mississippi.

**Photograph** by Hulton Archive/Getty Images

# CHARLEY PRIDE

**"I sang what I liked in the only voice I had."**
*Charley Pride*

In the 1950s, Sledge native Charley Pride listened to the Grand Ole Opry but was told he could never perform there. So, he pulled on a jersey and hit homers for the Negro American League. Between ballparks, he traded his bat for a guitar and entertained teammates. During a stop in Nashville, Chet Atkins recognized Pride's talent and offered him a contract with RCA Records. He quickly racked up three hits. There was only one catch. His race was kept secret. When he made his first public appearance, the stunned audience grew silent. But Pride's music prevailed, and supportive country fans lined up for autographs.

It took nearly 40 years, but in 1993, Pride was given the ultimate country music sign of respect. He was inducted into the Grand Ole Opry.

**Photograph** Charley Pride on The Johnny Cash Show (circa 1970). Photo courtesy ABC Photo Archives

# BOBBIE GENTRY

**"Chickasaw County child / You gonna be somebody someday."**

*lyrics by Bobbie Gentry*

Bobbie Gentry spent her childhood in poverty on her grandparents' Chickasaw County farm. When her family traded a cow for a piano, seven-year-old Gentry composed her first song and launched a career that would rattle the music industry. With a sultry voice, a survivor's sixth sense, and knock-em-dead beauty, Gentry was one of the first female country artists to write and produce her own material. And what great material it was. Her heavy lyrics were pulled from her edgy southern heritage, with hits that included "Mississippi Delta," "Okolona River Bottom Band," and the tragic "Ode to Billy Joe," in which she detailed Billy Joe McAllister's suicidal leap from the Tallahatchie Bridge.

**Photograph** by Michael Ochs Archive

# LEANN RIMES

**"I was raised as a southern woman, so I am polite,
have great manners, and know how to handle myself."**
*LeAnn Rimes*

While LeAnn Rimes may be known for her southern sensibilities, she's also made quite a name for herself with her musical talents. With the rare quality of perfect pitch, the Pearl native was singing by the age of two, performing live by age five, and recording her first album by age seven.

With strong parental support, Rimes has spent her entire life on stage — and her career is still going strong, as she continues to release chart-topping hits and perform flawlessly for enthusiastic audiences. With three Grammy Awards under her belt, this southern girl has a lot more to offer fans in the years to come.

**Photograph** by SGranitz

# MARTY STUART

Hillbilly rocker. Master string picker. Prestigious Grand Ole Opry member. Four-time Grammy winner. Platinum recording artist. Add to that six years as Johnny Cash's guitarist and five years as his son-in-law. Not bad for a boy from Philadelphia, Mississippi who taught himself to play guitar and mandolin and joined a bluegrass band at the age of 12. With dozens of Top 40 hits, a number one television show, and a public collection of music memorabilia and photography, Stuart continues to be the nation's foremost advocate for country music. He has served as president of the Country Music Foundation and has collaborated with the biggest names in the industry while staying true to his roots. In 2009, Mississippi's Neshoba County declared a Marty Stuart Day in honor of their small town boy who dared to pursue big dreams.

**Photograph** by Robert Knight Archive/Redferns

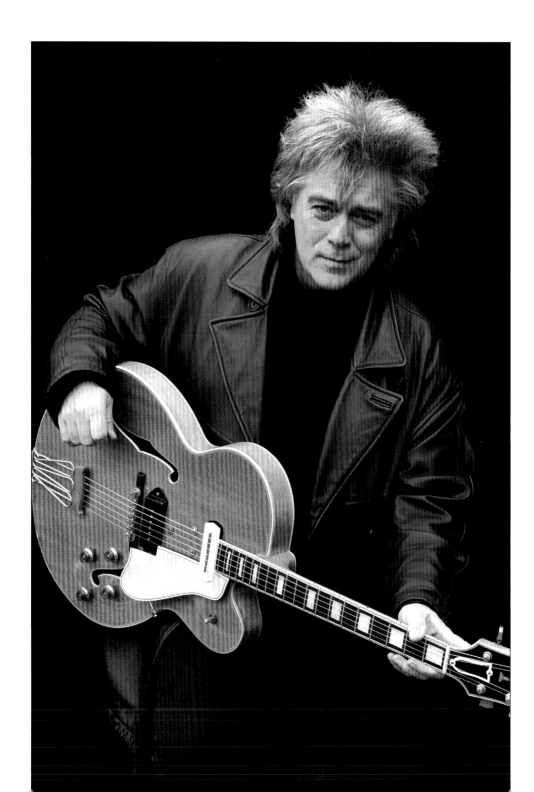

# TAMMY WYNETTE

**"The queen of country music."**
*New York Times*

What happens to a girl whose father dies, whose mother abandons her, and who's picking cotton by the age of eight? If she's born in Itawamba County, she might become the queen of country music. That's exactly what happened to Tammy Wynette, a beautician-turned-songstress who spent decades recording hits that gave voice to long-suffering working class women (think "Stand by Your Man"). Wynette explored personal struggles with raw truth and told a story with each emotional note. As she once said, you have to live it to sing it. And that's what Wynette did, always remaining a Mississippi girl at heart — even when she sang for the president, raising her designer gown to reveal her bare feet. From cotton fields to the White House lawn, Wynette made her own way and left a trail of awards, accolades, and lasting music in her path.

**Photograph** by GAB Archive/Redferns

# ROBERT JOHNSON

**"We all owe our existence, in some way, to Robert Johnson."**
*Robert Plant, Led Zeppelin*

Robert Leroy Johnson was born in Hazlehurst, Mississippi in 1911 and died a short 27 years later in Greenwood. He has been called "the most important blues singer that ever lived." He reportedly achieved his greatness by selling his soul to the devil at the crossroads. He influenced a generation of British musicians, including Eric Clapton, who called Johnson's music "the most powerful cry I think you can find in the human voice." Johnson is ranked as the fifth greatest guitarist of all time by *Rolling Stone* magazine.

Robert Johnson Studio Portrait, Hooks Bros., Memphis, circa 1935, © 1989 Delta Haze Corporation. All Rights Reserved. Used By Permission

# WILLIE DIXON

**"Blues are the root. The rest is the fruit."**

*Willie Dixon*

As a child, Vicksburg native Willie Dixon picked up on his mother's habit of speaking in rhyme. When he started to tinker with music, he converted poems into original songs. Dixon landed in a Mississippi prison farm as a teen. There, he was introduced to the blues. Dixon had two things going for him. He was big, and he could sing. But he used his physical strength to make an impact first. He moved to Chicago, became a heavyweight boxing champion, and served as Joe Louis' sparring partner. While in the gym, he harmonized with Leonard Caston, who brought him his first instrument. It was a tin can and string, but it was just enough to launch one of the most influential blues careers of all time and land a Mississippi boy in the Rock and Roll Hall of Fame.

**Photograph** by Paul Natkin/WireImage

# MOSE ALLISON

**"I don't know any musicians who don't love Mose Allison."**
*Bonnie Raitt*

Tippo native Mose Allison has recorded more than 40 albums and written more than 150 original songs. He is more popular among musicians than the public. In the 1960s, his music inspired The Yardbirds, Georgie Fame, and The Who. In an interview Allison was asked, "You were a social critic before Dylan; you were satirical long before Newman; you were rude long before Jagger; why aren't you a big star?" Allison responded: "Just lucky, I guess." His albums *Lessons for Living* and *Ever Since the World Ended* were both nominated for Grammy Awards. His original works have been recorded by Bonnie Raitt, The Who, Elvis Costello, Diana Krall, Van Morrison, and Leon Russell.

**Photograph** by David Redfern/Redfern

# CASSANDRA WILSON

**"One of the most beguiling sounds in jazz and blues."**
*The Sunday Times*

Classically trained on piano from the age of six, Jackson native Cassandra Wilson was blessed not only with musical talent, but also with supportive parents. As educators and musicians, her parents instilled in Wilson an affection for all types of music and encouraged her to learn multiple instruments. Wilson's versatility is unparalleled in today's jazz industry. Vocalist, songwriter, producer, and two-time Grammy winner, Wilson has already achieved monumental success; but jazz fans around the world are counting on much more to come from this Mississippi girl whose parents taught her to believe, "I think I can."

**Photograph** Wilson performs in Amsterdam, Netherlands. Photo by Frans Schellekens/Redferns

# BRANDY NORWOOD

Known professionally as the R&B singer Brandy, Brandy Norwood was born in McComb, Mississippi. Brandy is one of the bestselling female artists in history. Her recordings have sold over 25 million albums worldwide — and she has won six Grammy Awards. She has also been successful in film and television. She starred in the Emmy Award-winning TV film *Rodgers and Hammerstein's Cinderella* as Cinderella, starred in the sitcom *Moesha*, and had a prominent role in *I Still Know What You Did Last Summer*. In 2009, Brandy began her rap career under the name Bran'Nu.

**Photograph** by Gerard Burkhar/AFP/Getty Images

# LANCE BASS

Lance Bass was born in Laurel, Mississippi, grew up in nearby Ellisville and later lived in Clinton, until joining the pop group `N Sync. The group achieved overnight fame and sold more than 56 million records worldwide. Lance made guest appearances in several television shows and starred in the 2001 film *On the Line*. He played Corny Collins in the Broadway Musical *Hairspray* for six months in 2007, during which he released his autobiography, *Out of Sync*. Since he was a child, Bass had dreamed of going to space, so he began cosmonaut training in 2002. He was scheduled to fly on a mission in 2003, but his sponsorships fell through in the last stages of preparation.

**Photograph** by Dave Kotinsky

# FIVE BLIND BOYS OF MISSISSIPPI

The Five Blind Boys of Mississippi was a gospel ensemble that formed in 1936 at the Piney Woods School near Jackson, Mississippi. The long-standing members included Archie Brownlee, Joseph Ford, Lawrence Abrams, and Lloyd Woodard. Their single "Our Father" reached the Billboard R&B charts in the early 1950s (it was the first gospel record to make the charts). In the 1950s and 1960s, the Five Blind Boys became superstars, recording five albums and 27 singles — and they paved the way for Ray Charles and Stevie Wonder.

**Photograph** by Jan Persson/Redferns

# DICK WATERMAN

Dick Waterman — photographer, promoter, and writer — spent the early part of his career uncovering musical talent around Mississippi and the South. He founded Avalon Productions, the first booking agency for Blues artists, and gathered an impressive group of clients. He represented Son House, Skip James, Sam "Lightnin'" Hopkins, Booker "Bukka" White, and Mississippi John Hurt, among others. Waterman persuaded a young Bonnie Raitt, as well as Buddy Guy, to pursue careers in music (both are Rock and Roll Hall of Famers). After moving to Oxford in the 1980s, he began compiling his own collection (built over a 40-year period) of photographs of blues, country, jazz, and folk artists. His book *Between Midnight and Day: The Last Unpublished Blues Archive* was published in 2003, followed in 2005 by *B.B.King: Treasures*. The Oxford resident was inducted into the Blues Hall of Fame in 2000, an honor rarely bestowed on a non-performer.

**Photograph** courtesy of Dick Waterman (left) with B.B. King (right)

# SONNY BOY WILLIAMSON

Born on the Sara Jones Plantation in Tallahatchie County in 1908, Sonny Boy Williamson was one of the finest blues harp players who ever lived — as well as one of the greatest blues songwriters (his titles include "Fattening Frogs for Snakes"). He hosted The King Biscuit Time Radio Show, broadcast out of Helena, Arkansas. He was popular among British musicians. Williamson recorded with The Yardbirds, the Animals, and Jimmy Page. Legend has it that Ike Turner got his start (at the age of 11) playing piano for Williamson. Williamson's only major hit, "Don't Start Talking to Me," reached number three on the Billboard R&B charts in 1953.

**Photograph** courtesy Hulton Archive (Getty)

# CHARLIE MARS

Charlie Mars grew up in Laurel, and began writing songs there at the age of fifteen. He released three independent records before signing to V2 records in 2004. Rolling stone wrote of Mars' work, "Big, emotional rock from Mississippi" with "a knack for hooks and the hooks here have real barbs: they tug at you and just might draw some blood." He released his fifth effort *Like A Bird, Like A Plane* in 2009, and is currently recording his sixth album in Austin, Texas. Mars now lives in Oxford.

**Photograph** by Darin Back

# STEVE AZAR

**"Steve Azar rocked the house on our last tour."**

*Bob Seger*

Steve Azar's 2009 concert tour with Bob Seger was ranked number one by the concert-industry publication *Pollstar*. And the *Columbus Dispatch* wrote, "Azar passed the crucial test for an opening act: He held the attention of people who had never heard of him." A loyal country music performer, Azar's biggest hit to date is "I Don't Have to be Me (`Til Monday)," which reached number two in the U.S. country charts.

Azar, a Greenville native, is now starring on The Golf Channel's series, *Playing Lessons*. And Golf Digest ranks him (along with Vince Gill and Kenny G) as one the top five golfing musicians.

**Photograph** by Rusty Russell/Getty Images

# SAM COOKE

Sam Cooke was born in Clarksdale, Mississippi. The son of a Baptist minister, Cooke began singing in the church choir at the age of six. Between the years 1957-1965, Cooke had 29 Top 40 hits, including "Another Saturday Night," "Frankie and Johnny," "Chain Gang," "A Change is Going to Come," and "Twisting the Night Away." He died in Los Angeles at the age of 33.

**Photograph** courtesy Michael Ochs Archives/Getty Images

# SKIP JAMES & SON HOUSE

Skip James of Bentonia was one of the most influential Delta bluesmen. He recorded 26 songs in 1931, including the legendary "Hard Time Killing Floor Blues." Eric Clapton's band, Cream, recorded James' "I'm So Glad." His song "Devil Got My Woman" was retitled "Hellhound on My Train," and recorded by Robert Johnson.

Son House of Riverton was a preacher, cotton-picker, drunk, and Parchman inmate before he focused on the blues. Although little-known in his own lifetime, he is considered by many to be the "Father of the Delta Blues." It is said that after a teenage Robert Johnson heard House play, Johnson dropped the harmonica and picked up a guitar. Rediscovered in 1964 by Dick Waterman and others, House performed across the country, including a stop at Carnegie Hall in 1965. House was also a tremendous influence on Mississippi great Muddy Waters.

**Photograph** Skip James and Son House sit on set during a television show recording as part of the American Folk Blues Festival tour in Copenhagen, Denmark (circa 1967). Photo by Jan Persson/Redferns

# MUDDY WATERS

Muddy Waters (born McKinley Morganfield in Issaquena County) is widely regarded as "Father of the Chicago Blues." Waters' music has been recorded by Jimi Hendrix, AC/DC, Canned Heat, The Rolling Stones, and many others (he also helped Chuck Berry get his first record contract). He was awarded six Grammys before his death in 1983. Waters was ranked number 17 in *Rolling Stone* magazine's list of the 100 Greatest Recording Artists of All Time.

**Photograph** by Gems, Redferns

# PAUL OVERSTREET

Paul Overstreet is one of the most respected songwriters working in country music. The Newton native has written or co-written 27 Top Ten songs. He is the recipient of two Grammy Awards, as well as back-to-back CMA Song of the Year Awards. He has written number-one hits for Randy Travis and Blake Shelton, and Top Ten hits for The Judds and Kenny Chesney.

Overstreet co-wrote "Love Can Build a Bridge" by the Judds, and "Forever and Ever, Amen" by Randy Travis.

**Photograph** by Skip Bolen, WireImage

# MISSISSIPPI JOHN HURT

Mississippi John Hurt was a sharecropper for most of his life. Although he started playing the guitar at a young age and was a gifted musician, his music was largely overlooked until folk musicologists Tom Hoskins and Mike Steward brought Hurt to the attention of the contemporary music world. During the last three years of his life, Hurt toured the Northeast to overflow crowds (and even appeared on *The Tonight Show* with Johnny Carson). Hurt died in 1966 in Grenada, Mississippi.

**Photograph** courtesy of Michael Ochs Archives

# MICKEY GILLEY

Born in Natchez, Mississippi, Mickey Gilley had a string of 17 number one country hits — and he received the Record of the Year Award in 1976 from the Academy of Country Music for his song "Bring It On Home." Gilley struggled for years to get out from under the shadow of his famous cousin, Jerry Lee Lewis (he is also a cousin to former television evangelist Jimmy Swaggart).

Gilley was part owner of the largest nightclub in the world — the 5,000-seat Gilley's in Pasadena, Texas — featured in the film *Urban Cowboy*.

**Photograph** courtesy of Michael Ochs Archives

# MAC MCANALLY

Mac McAnally grew up in Belmont, Mississippi, where he played piano and sang in the Belmont First Baptist Church choir. One of the most respected songwriters in Nashville, he was voted Musician of the Year by the Country Music Association in 2008.

"Down the Road" (a duet with Kenny Chesney) hit number one on the country charts in 2009 (McAnally originally wrote and recorded the song in 1990). McAnally has written songs for many country music stars, including Jimmy Buffett. He has recorded 13 albums. In 2010, he was nominated for a Grammy Award.

**Photograph** by Rick Diamond, Getty Images Entertainment

# JOHN LEE HOOKER

Clarksdale native John Lee Hooker developed an important musical style known as "talking blues" — and introduced "boogie" to blues fans. Hooker recorded more than 100 songs in the 1950s and 1960s. His innovative techniques were copied by The Rolling Stones, The Yardbirds, Foghat, and ZZ Top. Hooker's 1989 album, *The Healer*, sold over one million copies. He also won a Grammy for the work. Like Turner, he was inducted into the Rock and Roll Hall of Fame in 1991.

**Photograph** by Paul Natkin/WireImage

# JIMMY REED

Mathis James "Jimmy" Reed was one of the most famous blues songwriters. The Dunleith native's songs were recorded by Elvis Presley, Bill Cosby, The Rolling Stones, and many others. He recorded 56 albums during his career. During his posthumous induction into the Rock and Roll Hall of Fame, it was noted that no one, other than B.B. King, so effectively reached black and white audiences in the 1950s and 1960s.

**Photograph** by Richard McCaffrey, Michael Ochs Archives

# IKE TURNER

Ike Turner started performing at the age of 11. He co-wrote (with James Cotton) what was very likely the first rock and roll hit record, *Rocket 88*. He orchestrated the early career of Tina Turner (their tumultuous relationship was depicted in the film *What's Love Got To Do With It*), including the five-million-selling single, "Proud Mary." He was inducted into the Rock and Roll Hall of Fame in 1991.

**Photograph** by Michael Ochs Archives/Getty Images

# CARY HUDSON

Cary Hudson first became recognized as a pioneer of a new music movement in the late eighties while joined in songwriting partnership with John Stiratt (Wilco) in The Hilltops, an alt-country band born out of Mississippi. When Stiratt left The Hilltops to play bass in Uncle Tupelo and then Wilco, Cary Hudson formed the widely-popular Blue Mountain that captured critical acclaim and gained cult status among its followers. After enjoying a long and successful run, and several popular releases on Roadrunner Records, Blue Mountain disbanded and Cary Hudson embarked on his solo career. With his solo releases, Cary Hudson has perfected the roots rock-n-roll tradition in a new, stripped down, grittier style that returns rock to its roots. His releases and performances have been well-received by critics and fans alike, proving that Cary Hudson can transition from pioneer to powerful solo songwriter and musician. His solo releases continue to redefine the music that launched a movement.

**Photograph** by Chad Edwards, MCE Photography

# JIMMIE RODGERS

**"The man that started it all."**

*Country Music Hall of Fame*

Jimmie Rodgers, the "Singing Brakeman," was the first country music star. His record, "Blue Yodel," sold more than one million copies in the 1920s. The Father of Country Music, Rodgers' career lasted a mere six years (though he recorded more than 110 songs). He died of tuberculosis at the age of 35.

Rodgers, a Pine Springs native, was one of the first inductees into the Country Music Hall of Fame. He is the only performer to be inducted into all four major music Halls of Fame.

# HOWLIN' WOLF

**"No one could match Howlin' Wolf for the singular ability to rock the house down to the foundation while simultaneously scaring its patrons out of its wits."**

*Music critic Cub Koda*

Born Chester Arthur Burnett, Howlin' Wolf stood six feet, six inches and weighed over 300 pounds. Wolf was widely popular in England (The Beatles, Eric Clapton, and The Rolling Stones were all fans). Known as the founder of the Chicago electric blues, Wolf recorded 67 albums. His final concert (with fellow Mississippian B.B. King) was held in Chicago in 1975. In 1997, a life-size statue was unveiled in his hometown of West Point, Mississippi.

**Photograph** by Robert Abbott Sengstacke, Archive Photos

# GLEN BALLARD

Glen Ballard's first job was as a gofer with Elton John's band. But that led to a gig playing piano, and eventually writing a song for Kiki Dee. It was the beginning of an extraordinary career in music, songwriting, and producing. The Natchez native has made many contributions to the music world: he co-wrote the Michael Jackson song "Man in the Mirror," he produced and co-wrote Alanis Morissette's album *Jagged Little Pill* (at that time, the best selling album *ever* by a female recording artist), and he has won a handful of Grammy Awards.

**Photograph** by Lester Cohen, WireImage

# EDDIE COTTON, JR.

Eddie Cotton, Jr. is an electric blues guitarist from Clinton, Mississippi. The son of a preacher, he started playing

guitar at the age of four. One of the best guitarists to emerge from Mississippi in decades, Cotton played the part of Robert

Johnson in a film by Los Angeles director Glen Marzano. Cotton's best known work is his 2000 album entitled *Eddie*

*Cotton: Live at the Alamo Theater.*

**Photograph** by Skip Bolen/WireImage for NARAS

# BO DIDDLEY

Rock and roll vocalist, guitarist, and songwriter Bo Diddley (Ellas Otha Bates McDaniel) was one of the first black performers to appear on the Ed Sullivan Show. He had a string of hits during the 1950s and 1960s, including "Sixteen Tons," "Pretty Thing," "Say Man," and "You Can't Judge a Book by the Cover." Diddley, a McComb native, originally studied classical violin, but after hearing John Lee Hooker, he moved to blues and R&B. When he started recording, he adopted the stage name Bo Diddley — slang for "mischievous child."

In 1986, Diddley was one of the inaugural class inducted into the Rock and Roll Hall of Fame. He also received the prestigious Grammy Lifetime Achievement Award.

**Photograph** courtesy New York Daily News Archive

# CONWAY TWITTY

Country music legend and Friars Point native Conway Twitty (Harold Lloyd Jenkins) came up with his stage name by looking at a roadmap and spotting Conway, Arkansas and Twitty, Texas. Twitty started out recording rock and roll at Sun Records (he had a number one hit, "It's Only Make Believe"). In 1965, he made the switch to country (the first major rock star to make the move). He had more number-one hits — 55 — than any other recording artist in any genre.

**Photograph** courtesy Michael Ochs Archives

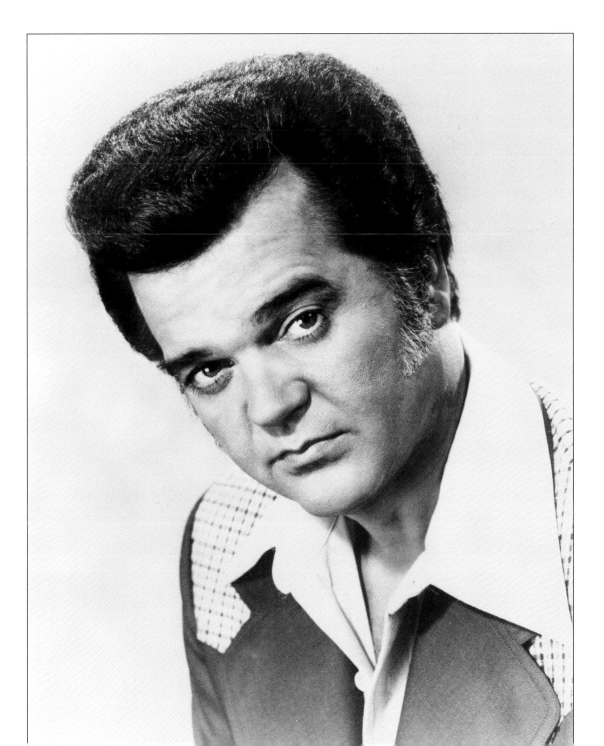

# BRUCE LEVINGSTON

One of the leading classical pianists in the country, Bruce Levingston was raised in Cleveland, Mississippi. His concerts at New York City's Carnegie Hall have received tremendous acclaim and his performances and recordings have been broadcast throughout the world. Because of his extraordinary talent, Levingston is often asked by composers to premiere their newest works. In 2001, Levingston founded the nonprofit organization Premiere Commission, which is dedicated to financing and promoting the work of living composers. In 2006, he received the Mississippi Arts Commission's Governor's Award for Artistic Excellence.

**Photograph** courtesy Bruce Levingston

# DELANEY BRAMLETT

**"I tried to present my music and I tried to make people feel good — I always felt that anybody that paid a dollar to see me, I'm gonna give them their dollar's worth."**

*Delaney Bramlett*

Delaney Bramlett's career as a musician, singer, songwriter, and producer spanned nearly five generations—beginning when he moved to California in the 1960s. A native of Pontotoc, Delaney is credited not only with teaching the Beatles' George Harrison how to play the slide guitar, but also with assisting and befriending music legend Eric Clapton. Throughout his thriving musical career, which he shared with his wife, Bonnie Bramlett, Delaney played and worked alongside J.J. Cale, Jimi Hendrix, John Lennon, Janis Joplin, and Jerry Lee Lewis.

In January 2011, Delaney Bramlett was inducted into the Mississippi Musicians Hall of Fame. He died on December 27, 2008.

**Photograph**  Delaney Bramlett (of Delaney & Bonnie) plays with Eric Clapton and George Harrison.
Photo by Jan Persson/Redferns

# JIMBO MATHUS

**"God bless Mississippi and pass the antiseptic."**
*Jimbo Mathus*

Jim Dickinson once called Jimbo Mathus "the singing voice of Huck Finn." Best known as the ringleader of the hyper-ragtime Squirrel Nut Zippers, Mathus is a prolific songwriter of born-in-the bone Southern music. He was first recorded at Sam Phillips Recording Service in Memphis in a group called The End in 1983. As a blues guitarist, he toured with the legendary Buddy Guy. In 2003 he founded a studio in Clarksdale and later relocated it to Como. His current band is The Tri-State Coalition, which he describes as "...a true Southern amalgam of blues, white country, soul and rock`n roll."

**Photograph** courtesy Jimbo Mathus

# NORTH MISSISSIPPI ALLSTARS

Composed of guitarist Luther Dickinson, his brother, drummer Cody Dickinson, and Chris Chew on bass, the North Mississippi Allstars's first release *Shake Hands with Shorty* was nominated for a Grammy Award for "Best Contemporary Blues Album." *51 Phantom* and *Electric Blue Watermelon* also received nominations in the same category. In 2001 the group won a Blues Music Award for "Best New Artist Debut." They released an album *Master of Disaster* with John Hiatt, with whom they have toured, and teamed with Robert Randolph and John Mediski to form "The Word." While the brothers continue to explore their music together, in 2007 Luther Dickinson also joined The Black Crowes as lead guitarist and Cody Dickinson began Hill Country Revue. Luther and Cody are the sons of legendary musician and producer Jim Dickinson.

**Photograph** by Getty

# JIM DICKINSON

Musician/producer Jim Dickinson was born in Arkansas, grew up in Memphis and, with his wife, Mary Lindsay, raised his family in Mississippi. Dickinson's career spanned from Sun Studios in the 1950s to winning a Grammy with Bob Dylan in 1997, to producing CDs by the Replacements, Big Star and dozens of other artists including his sons, Luther and Cody, the North Mississippi Allstars. Dickinson was highly sought as an "idea man" in the studio. As Bob Dylan wrote in his autobiography, "If you got Jim Dickinson, you don't need anybody else." Dickinson played piano with the Rolling Stones, backed Aretha Franklin, worked extensively with Ry Cooder, and can be heard on "City of New Orleans" by Arlo Guthrie, among numerous other recordings. He passed away on August 15, 2009.

In 2011, Dickinson was awarded a brass musical note on Beale Street in Memphis. His memoir, *The Search for Blind Lemon*, will be published posthumously. All this activity bears truth to his epitaph, "I'm just dead, I'm not gone."

**Photograph** Jim Dickinson outside Sun Studios. Photo by Ebet Roberts/Redferns   **Story** by Jim Dees

# THE TANGENTS

If you were staging an event in Mississippi anytime between 1981 and 1995 and booked The Tangents, your guests were assured you were serious about fun. Emerging from the Delta to bring authentic rhythm and blues to clubs and parties across the south, the band quickly found favor with their raw vocals, energetic musicianship and unerring sense of soul. Their versatility — covering Duke Ellington, the Beatles and Hank Williams in a single set — made them the "go-to" group for any occasion, earning their nickname, "Mississippi's House Band."

The Tangents never released an official album (bootleg cassettes continue to circulate) but have attained mythical status among those fortunate enough to experience them live. Saxophonist Charlie Jacobs died in 1997 but the surviving members still appear together on rare occasions. In their heyday, on certain rocking, sweaty evenings, it seemed, perhaps, at least for that one night, there was no other band.

**Photograph** courtesy Duff Durrough • **Story** by Jim Dees

# CAROLINE HERRING

**"Herring is a storyteller who happens to set her tales, woeful and happy, to music."**
*Delta Magazine*

Caroline Herring, a folk and country singer-songwriter from Canton, Mississippi, is swiftly gaining fame and recognition around the world. Her albums *Twilight*, *Wellspring*, and *Lantana* have received awards from NPR, *The Austin Chronicle*, and the *Atlanta Journal-Constitution*. "Mississippi's dense history and the shackles of its past are vividly present in Herring's songs," noted Craig Havihurst in the *Tennessean*.

Herring continues a busy tour schedule. Her latest album, *Little House Songs*, was released in 2011.

**Photograph** by Joel Silverman

# PINETOP PERKINS

Pinetop Perkins began playing blues in the 1920s, playing at house parties in his hometown of Belzoni, Mississippi. Perkins worked with many different artists throughout his career, as well as recording solo, but was perhaps most well known as the piano player in the Muddy Waters Band for twelve years. His solo career didn't really win him fame until later in life, and his work was nominated for Grammy awards in 1997, 2000, and 2005.

In 2005, Perkins was presented with a Grammy Lifetime Achievement Award.

**Photograph** by Gary Miller/FilmMagic

# R.L. BURNSIDE

Born in Harmontown, Mississippi, R.L. Burnside spent much of his early life working as a sharecropper and fisherman, only playing music for parties on the weekends. He moved to Chicago in the 1950s, but his career didn't take off and he headed back to Mississippi. In the 1990s, he appeared in the documentary *Deep Blues* and began recording for Oxford's Fat Possum Records. His album *A Ass Pocket of Whiskey* earned much praise from critics as well as music notables such as Bono and Iggy Pop.

Burnside recorded with Fat Possum until his death in 2005.

**Photograph** by Getty

# PETE FOUNTAIN

Pete Fountain started playing clarinet at an early age. Fountain, a Bay St. Louis resident, was heavily influenced first by Benny Goodman and then by Irving Fazola. Early on he played with the bands of Monk Hazel and Al Hirt.

Fountain became famous for his many solos on *The Lawrence Welk Show*. Welk once fired Fountain for "jazzing up" a Christmas number on the show.

Fountain has been the face of New Orleans jazz for years. After heart surgery in 2006 he performed at JazzFest, and helped reopen the Hollywood Casino post-Katrina.

He performed his last show at the Hollywood Casino on December 8, 2010.

**Photograph** by Getty

# GUY HOVIS

Born and raised in Tupelo, Guy Hovis has one of the more recognizable faces in America. He has been on national television for more than forty years beginning with the *Art Linkletter's House Party Show* on CBS in 1967. He has recorded fifteen albums, has been nominated as artist and producer of the year by the Gospel Music Association. He is also a member of the Mississippi Musicians Hall of Fame.

Throughout his career Guy has appeared on celebrity game shows, in national commercials, and on telethons for charities. Hovis is best known for the forty plus years he has been a regular member of the *Lawrence Welk Show* which is still aired on 280 public television stations with a weekly viewing audience of over 3 million.

# MARY WILSON

An original and enduring Supreme, Mary Wilson's roots began in Greenville. As a teenager in Detroit, she and future Supreme Florence Ballard teamed to become The Primettes, an alternative to the all-male The Primes, which later became the Temptations, featuring another Mississippi singer, David Ruffin. With Motown support the group eventually re-formed as The Supremes with the addition of Diana Ross. In 1964, they released "Where Did Our Love Go" and went on to make pop chart history with a string of hits. Throughout the tumultuous changes to befall the group, Mary Wilson remained a Supreme for its entire 18-year history. She went on to a career as a jazz and blues singer, a humanitarian and author of the best-selling autobiography, *Dreamgirl: My Life as a Supreme.*

**Photograph** (left to right) Mary Wilson, Diana Ross and Florence Ballard, of The Supremes. Photo by RB/Redferns

# ACE CANNON

**"Ace Cannon is the greatest saxophone player who ever lived."**
*Sam Phillips*

Born in Grenada, Ace Cannon learned to play the saxophone when he was just ten years old. He did some of his earliest recordings with Sun Records in the 1950s, and released his hit "Tuff" in 1962, which hit #17 on the Billboard charts. Known as the "godfather of the sax," Ace Cannon has been inducted into three music halls of fame and has been honored with the Ace Cannon Festival in Calhoun City since 2007.

**Photograph** by GAB Archive/Redferns

# LITTLE MILTON

James Milton Campbell, Jr., known as "Little Milton," was born in Inverness and raised in Greenville. As a teenager playing guitar in the local bars, he was discovered and signed by Ike Turner, who was a talent scout for Sam Phillips' Sun Records. After recording several singles and having no hits, he left Sun in 1955. Finally in 1962 his single "So Mean to Me" peaked at #14 on the Billboard R&B chart. In 1965 his album *We're Gonna Make It* produced two hit singles, "We're Gonna Make It," which broke through to the predominately white artist Top 40 Radio, and "Who's Cheating Who?" hit #4 on the R&B chart. *Grits Ain't Groceries* was released in 1969.

In 1998 he was inducted into the Blues Hall of Fame and won a W C. Handy Award.

**Photograph** by Getty

# JOE FRANK COROLLA

Hailing from Leland, Joe Frank Corolla (center) moved to Los Angeles in the 70s where he joined with Dan Hamilton (left) and Tommy Reynolds (right) to start the soft rock trio Hamilton, Joe Frank & Reynolds. Their song "Don't Pull Your Love Out" hit #4 on the Billboard charts in 1971 and sold over a million copies. It can also be heard in the film *When Harry Met Sally*.

During the late 60s in Mississippi, there was no place more exciting on a Saturday night than the "Battle of the Bands." Joe Frank and the Knights of Leland were the reigning champs.

**Photograph** of Hamilton, Joe Frank & Reynolds. Photo by Getty

# LEHMAN ENGEL

Lehmen Engel, born in Jackson in 1910, was one of the most successful Broadway conductors of the 20th century. He conducted countless Broadways classics such as *Oklahoma*, *Carousel*, *Show Boat*, and Gershwin's opera *Porgy and Bess*. He recorded scores for television shows and films, specializing in Shakespeare films. He conducted the music for *Hamlet*, *Twelfth Night*, *The Taming of the Shrew*, and *The Tempest*. Throughout his career, Engel won six Tony Awards and was nominated for four more. He was close friends with Pablo Picasso.

**Photograph** courtesy Millsaps-Wilson Library, Millsaps College

# BETTY EVERETT

*H*ow do you know if he loves you so? Even if the name Betty Everett is not well-known, her signature hit single "The Shoop Shoop Song (It's in His Kiss)" is recognized worldwide. Everett was born in Greenwood in 1939. At a young age she began to sing gospel and to play piano in church. After moving to Chicago to pursue secular music, in 1963 she was discovered by Vee-Jay Records and released a bluesy "You're No Good" (later a #1 hit for Linda Ronstadt). "The Shoop Shoop Song" followed and put Everett at #6 on the Billboard Hot 100 and #1 on the Cashbox R&B chart. She later recorded "Let it Be Me" with Jerry Butler, again a Cashbox #1 hit and a #5 U.S. hit. She won the BMI Pop Award in 1964 and then again in 1991. Her last live radio appearance was with the Chicago Blues Festival in which she was given a starring role and which aired live worldwide.

**Photograph** by Getty

# W.C. HANDY

W.C. (William Christopher) Handy wasn't the first musician to play the blues, but he is given credit for being the first to dress it up, take it out of the Mississippi Delta, push it through a horn, and show it off.

Handy was both an educated musician and a music educator. His fascination with the native music of the Mississippi Delta, and his enthusiasm for spreading the word, led to the greatest musical revolution.

Although he had a long and prolific career as an iconic musician and publisher, "St. Louis Blues" in 1914 and "Beale Street Blues" in 1916 were his most famous. In fact, before the release of "Beale Street Blues" and its subsequent popularity, the the famous Memphis street was actually named Beale Avenue.

**Photograph** W.C. Handy and Cab Calloway. Photo by Michael Ochs Archive.

# CHARLIE MUSSELWHITE

Although Charlie Musselwhite is identified as one of the first "white bluesmen" to come to prominence in the 1960s, he claims his Cherokee heritage. His musical schooling as a Memphis teenager during the birth of rock and roll shaped his sensibilities as a musician. Following the blues highway to Chicago, he hung out with blues greats such as Muddy Waters, Sonny Boy Williamson, Buddy Guy and became a lifelong friend of John Lee Hooker. After the release of his first successful album in 1966, *Stand Back! Here Comes Charley Musselwhite's Southside Band*, he moved to San Francisco where he became the top blues leader during the countercultural music scene. Known as a musician's musician, he has played on albums with Tom Waits, Bonny Raitt, The Blind Boys of Alabama, released over 20 albums, won 14 W. C. Handy Awards, and six Grammy nominations, as well as Lifetime Achievement Awards from the Monterrey Blues Festival and the San Javier Jazz Festival in Spain.

**Photograph** by Getty

# DAVID RUFFIN

David Ruffin, born Davis Eli Ruffin in Whynot, Mississippi, has one of the most heard voices in musical history; yet his individual fame was overshadowed by his involvement in the wildly successful musical group of the 1960s — The Temptations. Ruffin sang vocals on songs such as "My Girl" and "Ain't Too Proud to Beg," easily two of the group's most popular songs. Ruffin was inducted into the Rock and Roll Hall of Fame in 1989, and in 2008, he was ranked as one of the 100 Greatest Singers of All Time by *Rolling Stone* magazine. Marvin Gaye, fellow Motown artist, said of Ruffin's unique tenor vocals, "I heard in [his voice] a strength my own voice lacked."

**Photograph** by Getty

# HANK COCHRAN

**"Hank Cochran wrote three of the Top 100 country music songs of all time."**
*Country Music Television*

Ask any insider in the country music industry to name a songwriter who has influenced the genre, and they'll likely name Isola native Hank Cochran. Hundreds of country singers have gone straight to the Cochran catalog to find a sure hit, including stars Willie Nelson, Patsy Cline, Elvis Presley, Johnny Cash, George Strait, Brad Paisley, Ray Price, and LeAnn Rimes. In 1974, he was the first songwriter to be elected unanimously to the Nashville Songwriters Association's International Hall of Fame, and he's received dozens of BMI awards throughout the decades.

Perhaps he's able to write painfully poetic lyrics due to childhood challenges. At the age of nine, he was placed in a Memphis orphanage after his parents divorced. By 12, he had hitchhiked to New Mexico to work the oil fields. When he landed in Nashville, he became a full-time songwriter after co-writing Patsy Cline's hit "I Fall to Pieces." It was the start of a brilliantly creative career.

**Photograph** by Getty

# HARRY WHITE

**"Hearing saxophonist Harry White is like hearing the instrument with new, different ears."**
International music magazine *Das Orchester*

Harry White is widely regarded as one of the world's premier classical saxophonists. The Gulfport native is a guest performer with symphonies across the globe — and over one hundred original compositions have been created for White and his groups (including a Philip Glass concerto for the Rascher Saxophone Quartet when White was a member). White was the last protégé of renowned saxophonist Sigurd Rascher. At the age of seven, White was diagnosed with dyslexia. A teacher suggested he learn to play a musical instrument. White picked up the alto sax.

# WRITING & LITERATURE

# MARGARET WALKER ALEXANDER

**"I want my careless song to strike no minor key; no fiend to stand between my body's Southern song — the fusion of the South, my body's song and me."**

*Margaret Walker Alexander*

The Federal Writer's Project provided opportunities for some of the world's most renowned writers, including Mississippi's own Margaret Walker Alexander. After her book of poetry *For My People* earned her the Yale Award for Young Poets, she began teaching at Jackson State University, where she founded the Institute for the Study of the History, Life and Culture of Black People. Best known for her novel *Jubilee*, which tells the story of a slave, Alexander celebrated her African-American culture throughout her many works. She was awarded the Mississippi Lifetime Achievement Award for Excellence in the Arts and the White House Award for Distinguished Senior Citizens.

**Photograph** of *Jubilee* book signing, courtesy the Margaret Walker Alexander National Research Center

# LARRY BROWN

**"Larry Brown slapped his own fresh tattoo on the big right arm of Southern Lit."**

*The Washington Post*

Larry Brown began writing in his spare time when he was a firefighter and, after many rejections, published his first book, *Facing the Music* (1988), at the age of 37. The Tula native's books include *Dirty Work, Big Bad Love, Joe, Father and Son,* and *Fay.* His novels and short stories have been adapted for stage and screen. Brown's works are often associated with the literary styles of dirty realism or southern gothic. One critic described Brown's writing as "Southern-fried Greek tragedies filled with angry, deranged, and generally desperate characters who are fueled by alcohol and sex." *Men's Journal* reported, "Brown writes like a boxer — economical, crisp, wounding." And *The Washington Post Book World* noted, "He's one of the best we have."

In 2004, at the age of 53 — arguably at the height of his career — Brown died unexpectedly of heart failure.

**Photograph** Larry Brown reads from *Big Bad Love* in New York City. Photo by Gabe Palacio/ImageDirect

# SHELBY FOOTE

**"He shows promise, if he'll just stop trying to write Faulkner, and will write some Shelby Foote."**

*William Faulkner, on Foote to students at the University of Virginia*

A southerner at heart, and a loyal Mississippian, Shelby Foote wrote a strikingly objective historical narrative on the Civil War that propelled him into the national literary spotlight. Told with clarity (and never falling prey to nostalgia or romantic idealism of the war, or of the South), Foote's *The Civil War: A Narrative* secured his place as a major contributor to the American historical narrative.

Foote was born in Greenville, Mississippi, in 1916 to a declining aristocratic southern family (his paternal grandfather had gambled away much of the family's fortune by the time of Foote's birth). At the age of 15, Foote befriended another future Mississippi writer, Walker Percy. Foote and Percy went on to college together at Chapel Hill, where their lifelong literary friendship flourished. Foote's masterpiece, *The Civil War: A Narrative* (which took 20 years to write) rose to bestseller status in the early 1990s with the broadcast of Ken Burns' *The Civil War*. The documentary, in which Foote is a dominant presence, made the writer famous almost overnight: his great three-volume collection began to sell as many as 1,000 copies a day.

**Photograph** by Frederick M. Brown

# RICHARD FORD

**"A Babe Ruth of novelists, excelling at every part of the game."**

*The Washington Post*

Mississippi writer Richard Ford creates darkly lyrical, mystical worlds within major American cities, affluent suburbs, and wide-skied western towns. Although his work never ventures far from the realism of traditional plot and character, his richly textured sentences border on a new American sublime. Ford's language seduces readers into their own realities of time and space only to learn horrifying existential truths about life in America. There is very little redemption in the works of Richard Ford, only the faint hope that all is not quite as bad as it seems to be.

Born in Jackson, Mississippi, Ford spent many years living on Bourbon Street in New Orleans, where he made his first serious attempts at writing. When his first novel, *A Piece of My Heart*, did not sell very well, Ford gave up fiction writing to become a sports writer in order to earn a living. His breakthrough novel, *The Sports Writer*, catapulted Ford into the literary spotlight followed by the highly acclaimed story collection *Rock Springs* in 1987, which assured his position as one of the strongest writers of his generation. In 1995, he won the Pulitzer Prize for fiction with the release of his fifth novel, *Independence Day*.

Ford recently moved back to Oxford to teach in Ole Miss' MFA program in creative writing.

**Photograph** by Ulf Andersen

# ELLEN GILCHRIST

**"She taught us to write in our own voice."**

*Ellen Gilchrist on Eudora Welty*

As an escape from the pains of a divorce, Ellen Gilchrist enrolled in a writing class at Millsaps College. Gilchrist's teacher? Eudora Welty. "When I first read her, my mouth was hanging open because she wrote the way I and people I knew talked. It was a revelation to me."

Known for her complex heroines who fight against the restraints of southern society, the Vicksburg native has been compared to other southern greats like Tennessee Williams and Flannery O'Connor. Gilchrist is noted for her many works of fiction, poetry, and memoir. Her short story collection, *Victory Over Japan*, won the 1984 National Book Award for Fiction and she now has more than 17 books to her name. All thanks to another Mississippi writer who took time to encourage Gilchrist's talents.

**Photograph** by Andrew Kilgore

# BARRY HANNAH

**"The maddest writer in the USA."**

*Truman Capote*

Hannah was born in 1942 on Shakespeare's birthday in Meridian, Mississippi, and grew up in the small Mississippi town of Clinton. His deep South upbringing, albeit upper-middle class, informs all of his works in ways never quite seen before in American letters. His first novel, *Geronimo Rex*, published when Hannah was just 30 years old, is a perplexing, unorthodox coming-of-age novel that jerks the reader across genres and in and out of literary styles: psycho-punk, postmodernism, dirty realism, southern gothic, straight memoir, high modernism, pure fiction, and neo-primitivism. The contradictory categories ultimately render a complete, symmetrical literary whole. With this one work, Hannah secured his place among the strongest writers of his generation. In 1978, his reputation as a master of the short story was cemented in the collection *Airships*, now considered an American classic. In 1993, he published his magnum opus: the short story collection *Bats Out of Hell*, written as Hannah recovered from both alcoholism and the death of his father. His last work, *Yonder Stands Your Orphan*, is an incoherent masterpiece of the fragmented narrative that Hannah managed to complete in 2001 while in the throes of a death struggle with non-Hodgkin lymphoma.

Barry Hannah died of natural causes in Oxford, Mississippi, on March 1, 2010. He is buried in St. Peter's Cemetery in Oxford roughly two hundred yards from that other great American literary giant, William Faulkner.

**Photograph** by Nancy R. Schiff/Hulton Archive

# BETH HENLEY

**Meg:** *Why'd you do it, Babe? Why'd you put your head in the oven?*
**Babe:** *I don't know . . . I'm having a bad day.*

In Beth Henley's play *Crimes of the Heart*, three eccentric sisters reunite at Ole Grandaddy's House in Hazlehurst, Mississippi, after Babe shoots her abusive husband.  The reason Babe gave for the shooting?  "I didn't like his looks." Praised for its black humor, humanity, and spot-on regional voices,  the play went on to win the Pulitzer Prize in 1981. Five years later, a film version, starring Sissy Spacek, Jessica Lange, and Diane Keaton, earned Henley an Oscar nomination for Best Adapted Screenplay.

Beth Henley lives in California now with her son but continues to write plays and screenplays set in the South, such as *The Miss Firecracker Contest* (1980) and *Impossible Marriage* (1988).  So empathetic are her characters and so convincing is her dialogue that her work is often compared to another great Jacksonian, Eudora Welty.

**Photograph** Beth Henley at *Crimes of the Heart* Premiere. Photo by Jim Smeal • **Story** by Beth Ann Fennelly

# WILLIE MORRIS

**"Prose that is extraordinarily clean, flexible and incisive."**

*The New York Times Book Review*

Willie Morris wrote about the South like no other. Unabashedly sentimental, Morris' love of Mississippi, and his hometown of Yazoo City, is evident in his classics *Good Ole Boy*, *North Toward Home*, *My Dog Skip*, and *The Courting of Marcus Dupree*.

A college newspaper editor, baseball player, and Rhodes Scholar at the University of Texas, Morris soon ascended to the pinnacle of literary publishing. At the age of 32, he became editor-in chief of America's oldest magazine, *Harper's*. Morris was the eighth — and youngest — editor in the magazine's 117-year history. While at *Harper's*, Morris helped launch the careers of William Styron and Norman Mailer.

In the 1970s and 1980s, as writer-in-residence at the University of Mississippi, Morris brought his friends — among them Styron, George Plimpton, and Alex Haley — to Oxford, giving the town even more literary clout.

The film adaptation of *My Dog Skip* was released in 2000, starring Kevin Bacon, Diane Lane, and Frankie Muniz.

**Photograph** by David Rae Morris

# WALKER PERCY

**"Percy touches the rim of so many human mysteries."**

*Harper's*

It was a 1941 bout of tuberculosis that permanently altered the literary course of physician-turned-novelist Walker Percy. As Percy convalesced at the Truden Sanitarium amid the Adirondack Mountains, he discovered the works of the existential philosophers, most notably Danish thinker Soren Kierkegaard.

Percy is perhaps the most philosophical writer that America has produced in the past 50 years. His works, both fiction and non-fiction, explore post-war American culture, with a particular interest in the alienated individual in the decline of the Old South and the birth of the New South.

Following his father's suicide and the death of his mother two years later, Percy moved to Greenville, Mississippi to be raised by his paternal uncle, a distinguished attorney whose love of theology and literature had a profound effect on the would-be writer. In Greenville, Percy became friends with another literary aspirant, Shelby Foote. They went to college together at Chapel Hill, where Percy studied medicine. At the age of 45, Percy published his first novel, *The Moviegoer*, an instant commercial and critical success. The novel, which explores contemporary southern society, set the pace for the rest of his works.

# ALICE WALKER

**"Alice Walker is one of the most important, grieving, graceful
and honest writers ever to come into print."**

*June Jordan*

Alice Walker came to Jackson, Mississippi in 1966 to work for the Legal Defense Fund of the NAACP. There Walker took depositions from blacks who had been evicted from their homes. The reason: they tried to register to vote.

In 1968, Walker was named writer-in-residence at Mississippi's Jackson State University. She sharpened her writing skills and made careful observations about the characters and events around her. Those years in Jackson helped shape one of America's most influential writers.

In 1983, *The Color Purple* won the National Book Award and the Pulitzer Prize for Fiction (a first for an African-American woman). Walker's books have since sold more than 10 million copies and have been translated into more than two dozen languages.

**Photograph** of Alice Walker in her Jackson apartment ©1982 Christopher R. Harris. All rights reserved.

# RICHARD WRIGHT

**"Wright was one of the people who made me conscious of the need to struggle."**
*Amiri Baraka*

Born on a plantation outside Natchez (Roxie, Mississippi), Richard Wright overcame staggering obstacles to become one of America's most important writers. Wright's father was an illiterate sharecropper who abandoned his family when Wright was young. As a result, Wright spent time in an orphanage and bounced around to various family members throughout his childhood, including an uncle who was killed by a lynch mob while Wright was in his care. Due to his unstable home life, Wright received an inconsistent education that ended in ninth grade. Poverty. Racism. Abandonment. Wright had every reason to be angry and bitter. Instead, he moved to Chicago, spent as much time as possible reading library books, and started to write. His first novel, *Native Son*, depicted black urban ghetto life with brutal honesty. He went on to publish several pivotal works about America and race relations.

**Photograph** courtesy Hulton Archive

# ACE ATKINS

**"Ace Atkins can write rings around most of the names in the crime fiction field."**

*Elmore Leonard*

With a father in the NFL, a name like "Ace," and a cover photo on *Sports Illustrated* for playing on the undefeated Auburn Tigers football squad, you'd think Atkins would have led a life of sports. After all, O.J. Simpson taught him to high-five when he was a young boy. Despite his talents on the field, Atkins chose to put down the football and pick up the pen. He moved to Florida and worked as a crime reporter for *The Tampa Tribune*. The job provided plenty of material for his first novel, *Crossroad Blues*, and many stories thereafter. After being selected as a Pulitzer Prize finalist for a series he wrote for the paper, Atkins left the steady paycheck for life as a full-time novelist. He now lives on a farm in Water Valley and is the author of nine novels, including *The Ranger*, the debut novel in the Quinn Colson series, from G.P. Putnam's Sons.

After the death of prolific crime writer Robert B. Parker, Atkins was asked by the Parker family to take over writing the wildly popular Spenser crime series. Joan Parker, Mr. Parker's widow, said she was "delighted that the world of Spenser will live on in the capable, talented hands of such a gifted writer."

**Photograph** by Jay E. Nolan, © Carrefour, Ltd. 2008

# HOWARD BAHR

**"Bahr writes with eloquence and tender humanity."**
*Southern Living*

Howard Bahr grew up in Meridian, Mississippi. From 1982-1993 he was curator of Rowan Oak, the William Faulkner homestead and museum in Oxford. Bahr's first novel, *The Black Flower*, was a *New York Times Book Review* Notable Book and received the Harold D. Vursell Award from the American Academy of Arts and Letters. He followed with *The Year of Jubilo*, *The Judas Field*, and *Pelican Road*. A reviewer for the *New York Times* wrote of Bahr, "Not since James Agee has someone made the southern night so alive."

**Photograph** courtesy Lemuria Books

# FREDERICK BARTHELME

**"Frederick Barthelme is a master."**

*The New York Times*

Aguru of the high postmodernism fiction movement of the late 1960s and 1970s, Frederick Barthelme has carved a deep niche in contemporary literature. His works include *The Brothers, Rangoon,* and *Elroy Nights.* It has been said that a rotisserie chicken helped him understand that he needed to write about ordinary people (Barthelme is arguably the father of the literary movement known as K-mart realism). Barthelme lives in Hattiesburg.

**Photograph** courtesy Graphic House, Archive Photos, Getty Images

# STEPHEN AMBROSE

Dr. Stephen Ambrose was a renowned historian and acclaimed author of more than 30 books. Among his New York Times bestsellers are: *Nothing Like It in the World, Citizen Soldiers, Band of Brothers, D-Day - June 6, 1944,* and *Undaunted Courage.*

He was not only a great author, but also a captivating speaker, with the unique ability to provide insight into the future by employing his profound knowledge of the past. His stories demonstrate how leaders use trust, friendship and shared experiences to work together and thrive during conflict and change. His philosophy about keeping an audience engaged is put best in his own words:

"As I sit at my computer, or stand at the podium, I think of myself as sitting around the campfire after a day on the trail, telling stories that I hope will have the members of the audience, or the readers, leaning forward just a bit, wanting to know what happens next."

Ambrose died October 13, 2002 at the age of 66 in Bay St. Louis.

**Photograph** by Acey Harper/*Time & Life* Pictures

# D.C. BERRY

**"Playing music is really about listening, painting is really about seeing,
and writing is really about reading."**

*D.C. Berry*

While the choir sang and the collection plate was passed, a teenaged David Chapman Berry had a religious experience: he became a poet. Berry credits his early literary leanings simply "to boredom in church."

Born in Vicksburg and raised in Greenville, Mississippi, Berry went on to work at General Motors in Detroit. In 1966, he was drafted into the Army, serving as a medic. A stint in Vietnam yielded the poems that would become his first book, *Saigon Cemetery*. After the war, he returned to the states and received his Ph.D. from the University of Tennessee.

As a professor and poet, D.C. Berry has received many distinguished awards, including three Excellence-in-Teaching awards from the University of Southern Mississippi, the Charles Moorman Distinguished Professor in Humanities award from the University of Southern Mississippi, the *Florida Review* Editor's Prize, the Southern Federation of State Arts Agencies Poetry Award, and the Mississippi Institute of Arts and Letters Award.

Berry continues to write every day — and he is now raising money to help support students in MFA programs.

**Photograph** by Mike Stanton

# JILL CONNER BROWNE<sub>i</sub>

**"You are gonna be so mesmerized by our utter fabulosity."**
*From the O-fficial Sweet Potato Queen Website*

Born in Tupelo, Mississippi, Jill Conner Browne swept the nation with her Sweet Potato Queens® series, *The Sweet Potato Queens Book of Love* and *God Save the Sweet Potato Queens*. Browne's alter ego struck a chord with women (and some men) worldwide, which inspired groups to create their own "sisterhoods" of Sweet Potato Queens (over 6,000 chapters in 22 countries). The original Sweet Potato Queens (of which Browne herself is a founding member) gather in Jackson, Mississippi. More than three million copies of her books are in print.

**Photograph** by Photo by Tom Joynt, © SPQ, Inc.

# WILL CAMPBELL

Will Davis Campbell — activist, writer, and Baptist minister — is the author of nearly two dozen books. Campbell was an early supporter of civil rights in the South. His autobiographical work *Brother to a Dragonfly* was a finalist for the National Book Award in 1978.

 The son of a farmer from Amite County, Campbell was ordained as a minister by the age of 17. A self-described "steeple dropout" and "bootleg preacher and freelance civil rights activist," Campbell's life work has been centered around a theme of reconciliation. His book, *And Also With You: Duncan Gray and the American Dilemma*, covered the career of Mississippi Episcopal Bishop Duncan Gray, Jr. (Campbell and Gray, who are friends, are both known for their ministry of inclusion, not exclusion).

 Campbell was the inspiration for the late cartoonist Doug Marlette's character "Will B. Dunn" in his nationally syndicated comic strip, *Kudzu*.

During the aftermath of Dr. Martin Luther King's Assassination, Will D. Campbell (right) and Ralph Abernathy (left)
**Photograph** by Henry Groskinsky, *Time & Life* Pictures, Getty Images

# ELLEN DOUGLAS

**"Some people were simply born to write. Ellen Douglas is just such a writer."**
*Richard Ford*

Few writers frame their works in the landscapes and characters of Mississippi as poignantly as Ellen Douglas. Few writers handle the problems of race relations in Mississippi with such accuracy, candor, and grace. Perhaps Douglas' greatest contribution to contemporary literature is her ability to explain, through works of supreme fiction, the true nature of what it means to exist in Mississippi regardless of race.

Ellen Douglas (whose real name is Josephine Haxton) was born in Natchez, Mississippi, in 1921. She published her first novel, *A Family's Affair*, at the age of 40 to much acclaim. *A Family's Affair* was deemed one of the best novels by *The New York Times* in 1962, and was followed by *Black Cloud, White Cloud*, considered one of the top five novels of 1963 by *The New York Times*. She published *Apostles of Light* in 1973, which garnered a nomination for The National Book Award. Her 1988 collection, *Can't Quit You Baby*, is considered by many critics to be her masterpiece.

From 1979 until 1983, she was the writer-in-residence at the University of Mississippi, where the legendary Larry Brown was her student. Brown gave her credit for teaching him what it really means to write a story.

**Photograph** courtesy Noel Workman

# BETH ANN FENNELLY

**"Beth Ann Fennelly's poems are genuinely outstanding."**
*Harvard Review*

Beth Ann Fennelly won a 2003 National Endowment for the Arts Award, as well as the prestigious 2006 United States Artist Grant. She's published three books of poetry, all from W. W. Norton. Her first collection, *Open House,* won The 2001 Kenyon Review Prize, the GLCA New Writers Award, and was a Book Sense Top Ten Poetry Pick. Fennelly followed with *Tender Hooks* and *Unmentionables*. Former Poet Laureate of the United States Robert Hass called Fennelly's poetry "an immensely lively performance." *Great With Child*, a book of nonfiction, was published by Norton in 2006. Her poems have been reprinted in *Best American Poetry 1996, 2005*, and *2006, Contemporary American Poetry*, *The Penguin Book of the Sonnet*, *The Pushcart Prize*, and *Poets of the New Century*. She won a Fulbright in the spring of 2009.

Fennelly, who directs the MFA program in creative writing at the University of Mississippi, was selected as the 2011 Outstanding Liberal Arts Teacher of the Year. She lives in Oxford, Mississippi, with her husband, fiction writer Tom Franklin.

Fennelly and Franklin are collaborating on a novel. This after collaborating on three small humans.

**Photograph** by Jon Cancelino

# ANN FISHER-WIRTH

**"Sweet, rank, proud, precise, unafraid of either deep pain or deep joy . . ."**
*Rick Bass*

One of the strongest of the ecopoets in America, whose earth-bound poems have been described as "Mississippi organic," Ann Fisher-Wirth has lived in Oxford, Mississippi for over 20 years. Her collections of poems include *Blue Window*, *Five Terraces*, and *Carta Marina*, and the chapbooks *The Trinket Poems*, *Walking Wu-Wei's Scroll*, and *Slide Shows*. Former U.S. Poet Laureate Robert Hass has written of her work, "Very few poets have written 'the autobiographical lyric' with such fierce and stinging accuracy." Fisher-Wirth's awards include a Malahat Review Long Poem Prize, the Rita Dove Poetry Award, the MIAL Poetry Award, two MAC Fellowships, nine Pushcart nominations, and a Pushcart Special Mention. She has held a senior Fulbright to Switzerland and a Fulbright Distinguished Chair award to Sweden. She teaches and directs the environmental studies minor at the University of Mississippi; she also teaches yoga in Oxford. She is coediting a contemporary anthology of ecopoetry, forthcoming from Trinity University Press.

**Photograph** by Houston Cofield

# TOM FRANKLIN

**"I am amazed by Tom Franklin's power . . . I'm reminded, by the evocative strength
of the prose and the relentlessness of the imagination, of Faulkner."**
*Philip Roth*

Before he sat down to write stories, Tom Franklin worked as a heavy equipment operator at a sandblasting factory, a construction inspector in a chemical plant, a clerk at a hospital morgue, and a cleaner at a hazardous waste site. Franklin is the author of four novels, a short story collection, and the critically acclaimed novella, *Poachers*. A critic for *The Dallas Morning News* wrote, "If Flannery O'Connor and Raymond Carver had produced a love child, he might have been Tom Franklin." His stories have been selected for the anthology *New Stories from the South*. *Poachers* was included in the anthology *Best Mystery Stories of the 20th Century*, as well as *Best Noir Stories of the Century*. Franklin's new novel, *Crooked Letter, Crooked Letter*, was a *New York Times* bestseller in hard cover and paperback. Thus far, *Crooked Letter* has won the *Los Angeles Times* Book Prize for Mystery/Thrillers, The Alabama Library Association prize, the Willie Morris Prize for Southern Fiction. It has been nominated for the Edgar Allen Poe Award for Best Novel and the SIBA Book of the Year. Most recently, *Crooked Letter* has been nominated for the Anthony Award, the Barry Award, the Hammett Award and England's Gold Dagger Award. *Crooked Letter* has also been optioned for film.

Franklin is an assistant professor of creative writing at Ole Miss. He lives in Oxford with his wife, the poet Beth Ann Fennelly, and their three children.

**Photograph** by Maude Schuyler Clay

# THOMAS HARRIS

Thomas Harris, who grew up in the small town of Rich, Mississippi, achieved great success as a novelist, specializing in crime and horror. He is best known for his Hannibal Lecter series: *Red Dragon*, *The Silence of the Lambs*, *Hannibal*, and *Hannibal Rising*. The novels were eventually adapted to the screen (the films starred Anthony Hopkins as Dr. Hannibal Lecter). Despite the dark nature of his books, Harris' agent Morton Janklow says of him: "He's one of the good guys . . . he has these old-fashioned manners, a courtliness you associate with the South."

**Photograph** by Louis Monier/Gamma-Rapho

# CHARLAINE HARRIS

**"Never a dull moment."**
*Los Angeles Times*

Charlaine Harris, best known for her mystery fiction and urban fantasy novels, was born in Tunica, Mississippi. Her series *The Southern Vampire Mysteries* inspired the hit HBO series *True Blood*, which premiered in 2008. Harris' novels have been honored with the highest awards for mystery writers. She's also hit the *New York Times* bestseller list repeatedly.

**Photograph** Charlaine Harris arrives at the premiere of HBO's *True Blood* Season 3 in Hollywood. Photo by Michael Buckner

# GREG ILES

Greg Iles has produced eight *New York Times* bestselling novels, which have been published in more than 20 countries and translated into a dozen languages. He received the Mississippi Author's Award for Fiction and the Bertelsman Award for New Fiction for his novel *Black Cross*. David Pitt, of *Booklist*, noted, "If Iles has a trademark, a single literary feature that identifies him, it's his intriguing, ordinary-people-in-extraordinary-situations premises that hook readers immediately, forcing us to read on."

**Photograph** Greg Iles (left) and Stephen King (right) perform with the Rock Bottom Remainders New York City. Photo by Evan Agostini

# LEWIS NORDAN

**B**orn in Forest, Mississippi and raised in Itta Bena, Lewis Nordan waited until he was 45 to begin writing. His collections of short stories, including *Welcome to the Arrow-Catcher Fair*, *The All-Girl Football Team*, and *Music of the Swamp*, place Nordan in the same tradition as Faulkner, O'Connor, and Welty. Nordan's stories take place in fictional southern towns — no doubt inspired by his upbringing in Itta Bena. His novel *Wolf Whistle* won the Southern Book Award, as well as the Notable Book Award from the American Library Association.

**Photograph** courtesy Algonquin Books

# KATHRYN STOCKETT

As a fledgling writer, Kathryn Stockett sat quietly in Jackson's Eudora Welty library flipping through old newspapers and telephone directories to document life in 1962 Mississippi. She could never imagine where this research would lead her.

The Help finished as the fourth bestselling work of fiction of 2009 with more than three million copies sold — unheard-of numbers for a first-time author. The novel has been a must-read for book clubs across the country and The Huffington Post called The Help a modern-day To Kill A Mockingbird.

The film adaptation of the novel (produced by Steven Spielberg's Dreamworks Studios) was a summer hit in 2011, and book sales show no sign of slowing down. But Kathryn Stockett didn't write The Help to become a bestselling author. She wrote it because she missed the voice of her friend Demetrie. There is no better reason, no better motive, to put words on a page. More than three million readers will attest to that.

**Photograph** Kathryn Stockett at the Galaxy National Book Awards at BBC Television Centre in London. Photo by Mike Marsland

# DONNA TARTT

**"Highly entertaining!"**
*Publisher's Weekly*

A student of literary giants Barry Hannah and Willie Morris, Donna Tartt was born in Greenwood, Mississippi, and raised in nearby Grenada. Her most famous work, *The Secret History*, has sold millions of copies since its publication in 1992. Tartt's follow-up novel, *The Little Friend*, was published a full decade later. "I've written only two novels, but they're both long ones, and they each took a decade to write," Tartt said. "I'd rather write one good book than ten mediocre ones," she added.

Willie Morris said, "Donna Tartt is one of the strongest women writers of contemporary literature."

**Photograph** by Ulf Andersen, Getty Images Entertainment

# NATASHA TRETHEWEY

**"*Native Guard*, with all its beauty of feeling and form,
leaves its readers panting for Trethewey's next book."**

*Booksense*

Gulfport native Natasha Trethewey is a rising star in the poetry world. Her first collection, *Domestic Work* (2000), won the inaugural Cave Canem Poetry Prize, a 2001 Mississippi Institute of Arts and Letters Book Prize, and the 2001 Lillian Smith Award for Poetry. Her second collection, *Bellocq's Ophelia* (2002), received the 2003 Mississippi Institute of Arts and Letters Book Prize, was a finalist for both the Academy of American Poets' James Laughlin and Lenore Marshall prizes, and was named a 2003 Notable Book by the American Library Association. Her most recent collection is *Native Guard*, for which she won the 2007 Pulitzer Prize in Poetry.

**Photograph** by Logan Mock-Bunting

# BRAD WATSON

**"The best thing to come out of the South since *A Confederacy of Dunces*."**

*Gregory Rabassa, on Watson's* The Heaven of Mercury

Brad Watson, acclaimed writer of short stories, was born in Meridian, Mississippi. After a brief attempt at acting, Watson attended Mississippi State University. He has written three books, *Last Days of the Dog-Men*, *The Heaven of Mercury*, and *Aliens in the Prime of Their Lives*. He received the Sue Kaufman Prize for First Fiction from the American Academy of Arts and Letters, and his short stories have been published in *The New Yorker*. He has taught creative writing at the University of Alabama, Ole Miss, University of West Florida, Harvard University and, now, at the University of Wyoming.

**Photograph** by Rickey Yanaura

# CLAUDE WILKINSON

**"Wilkinson immerses the reader in a reverie of such brilliance
that one no longer exists in the world of opposites."**

*Bookpage*

Claude Wilkinson paints vivid landscapes of rural Mississippi both on canvas and the page — striking glimpses of a pastoral South dotted with hunters and their "speckled bird dogs," migrating geese, religious archetypes, and poisonous snakes.

In 1998, Wilkinson, a Nesbit native, received the prestigious Naomi Long Madgett Poetry Award, resulting in the publication of his first book, *Reading the Earth*. In 2000, at the invitation of Barry Hannah, Wilkinson became the first poet to serve as the University of Mississippi's John Grisham writer-in-residence.

Wilkinson's poetry — often called a cross between Wordsworth and Frost — is an intoxicating encapsulation of the natural landscapes of the northwestern hill country of Mississippi. His works give the reader a tactile experience of the natural world. Wilkinson's second collection, *Joy in the Morning*, continued his lyrical investigation of redemption through suffering within the context of nature.

His third collection of poems, *Marvelous Light*, was published in 2010.

**Photograph** by Bruce Newman

# STEVE YARBROUGH

**"Steve Yarbrough is wickedly observant, funny, cynical, evocative, and he possesses a gift that cannot be taught: he can tell a story."**

*John Grisham*

Born in Indianola, Mississippi, Steve Yarbrough is the author of five novels and three collections of short stories. A PEN/Faulkner finalist, he has received the Mississippi Authors Award, the California Book Award, the Richard Wright Award, and an award from the Mississippi Institute of Arts and Letters.

Jill McCorkle said, "Steve Yarbrough is a masterful storyteller — one of our best." Yarbrough's most recent novel, *Safe from the Neighbors*, was published by Knopf. He teaches creative writing at Emerson College in Boston.

**Photograph** by Antonina Yarbrough

# JACK PENDARVIS

**"Young Pendarvis writes gutbusting, high wit so very rare in these dumb ass greedy times.
You general readers are in for the longest laughs of the early century."**

*Barry Hannah*

Born in Bayou Le Batre, Alabama (yes, of Forrest Gump fame), Jack Pendarvis is regarded as one of the funniest writers working today. Pendarvis, a columnist for *The Oxford American* and *The Believer*, also serves as writer-in-residence at the University of Mississippi.

At a literary reading in Oxford, he opted not to read, but rather to sing Broadway show tunes. *Publishers Weekly* wrote, "His characters are quirky and grotesque, infuriating and hilarious." One such character, in an attempt to woo a beautiful receptionist, asked if she'd like to smell the tooth he lost the night before. His creations blurt out lines like —
"I am not the candidate with both kidneys."

Pendarvis' books include *Your Body is Changing*, *The Mysterious Secret of the Valuable Treasure* and *Awesome*.

**Photograph** by Bruce Newman

# JOHN PRITCHARD

**"Underneath this violent language and narrative, there is a sweet truth. It deserves to be read."**
*Harry Crews, about* Junior Ray

John Pritchard grew up in the Mississippi Delta, a place of dark and elemental myth that inspired him to write. Barnes and Noble named his debut novel *Junior Ray* one of their Top Ten Sensational Debut Novels for 2005. He followed that with a sequel, *Yazoo Blues*, in 2008. The third book in the Junior Ray series, *Sailing to Alluvium* will appear in 2012. He currently lives in Memphis, where he has taught college-level English — often in knickers — for most of the last thirty-two years.

Pritchard said, "I was a high-forceps delivery, pulled from my mother by force in an attempt to save her life and to perhaps forfeit mine. I survived and so did she. As a result I have no occiput at all, am exceedingly high-strung, and have led a desperately neurotic existence. All in all I seem to be quite fine. My mother never got over it. The event, itself, and, later, having to deal with me was all a bit too much. I bear survivor's guilt and have never found philosophy to be the consolation it was to Marcus Aurelius."

# JERE HOAR

**"I did feel the rumble of newspaper presses through the soles of my shoes when I was a boy."**

*Jere Hoar*

The son of an editor/publisher, Jere Hoar literally "grew up" in the newspaper business. Following in his father's footsteps, Hoar received a Ph.D. in mass communications from the University of Iowa and joined the Journalism Department of the University of Mississippi in 1956. During his 36-year tenure, Hoar developed and taught 19 different undergraduate and graduate courses, producing a veritable league of nationally recognized journalists and receiving a litany of awards and honors for his teaching.

After years of publishing short stories in literary journals and magazines, his first collection of fiction, *Body Parts*, was published when Hoar was 67 years old. The collection, named a "Notable Book of the Year" by the *New York Times*, received immediate critical acclaim. At the age of 73, Hoar published his first novel, *The Hit*, which won the Independent Publisher Award for best suspense/thriller novel of the year. His books are bestsellers in Poland.

A life-long southerner, Hoar lives on a farm near Oxford, Mississippi.

# STARK YOUNG

**"If anything is clear, it is that we can never go back, and neither this essay nor any intelligent person I know in the South desires a literal restoration of the Old South."**

*Stark Young*

The son of a Confederate soldier, Young was born in Como, Mississippi, in 1881. He entered the University of Mississippi at 15 and in 1902 was awarded a Master of Arts degree in English Literature at Columbia University. As a southern transplant in New York City, Young melded his small town upbringing with cosmopolitan life, a cultural contrast he would explore extensively as a writer. Young's deep connection to Mississippi and agrarian culture surfaced in his poems, plays, criticisms and novels.

After stints writing and editing for *The New Republic*, *Dial*, the *North American Review*, and *Theatre Arts Review*, Stark contributed to one of America's great literary movements of the 20th century — the Southern Agrarians. Stark's take on Southern Agrarianism is chronicled in the movement's seminal anthology, *I'll Take My Stand*. His most influential work, *So Red the Rose*.

**Photograph** courtesy Library of Congress

# DEAN FAULKNER WELLS & LAWRENCE WELLS

Dean Faulkner Wells and Lawrence Wells made great partners — as spouses and as literary figures. Together they operated Yoknapatawpha Press, a publishing house that features Southern writers. They also created the Faux Faulkner competition, which encouraged writers to parody William Faulkner's (uncle of Dean) unique writing style, themes or plots. Their home, where William Faulkner wrote *Absalom, Absalom*, has been a gathering place for aspiring writers.

Both talented authors, Lawrence has written two novels, *Rommel and the Rebel* and *Let the Band Play Dixie*, while Dean wrote and edited a number of books, including her memoir *Every Day by the Sun: A Memoir of the Faulkners*, published by Crown in 2011. Dean Faulkner Wells passed away in July of 2011 — the day she and Lawrence put the final touches on a collection of essays they co-authored.

**Photograph** Dean Faulkner Wells and Lawrence Wells at the launch event for *Every Day by the Sun: A Memoir of the Faulkners*.

# JONATHAN MILES

**"A crisp yowl of a first novel."**
*Publishers Weekly*

Jonathan Miles' debut novel, *Dear American Airlines*, electrified the literary world. A *New York Times Book Review* Notable Book of the Year selection, the book was called "funny, irreverent and heartbreaking" by Elizabeth Gilbert. Mark Richard called it "a pitch-perfect portrait." And Jim Harrison wrote, "A rough and wild ride. I loved this novel, which is strong medicine indeed."

Miles' work has been anthologized in the *Best American Sports Writing* and the *Best American Crime Writing* — and his stories have appeared in *GQ*, *The New York Observer*, and the *Oxford American*.

A protégé of Larry Brown, Miles has been called a major new talent in American fiction. Readers everywhere await his next novel.

**Photograph** by Leah Overstreet

# VISUAL ARTISTS

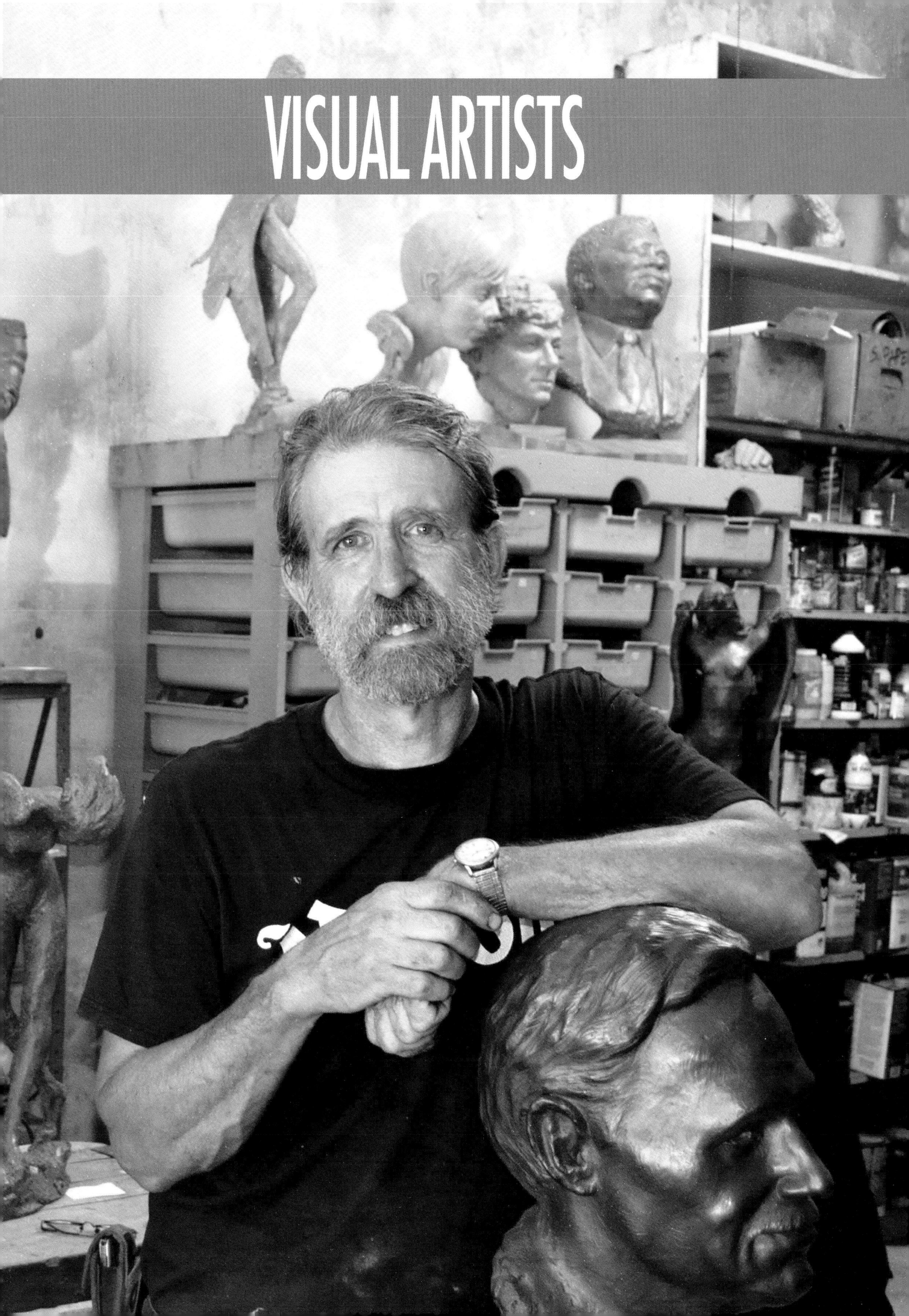

# GEORGE OHR

POTTER

**"No two pieces alike."**
*George Ohr*

George Ohr, the so-called "Mad Potter of Biloxi," was born in Biloxi, Mississippi. His experimental work in ceramics established him as forerunner of the Abstract Expressionist movement that took place in the early and mid-20th century. His unique style, with thin walls and obscure shapes, has never been properly replicated using a pottery wheel — the method that Ohr used. Much of the clay that he used to construct these pieces was dug directly from the Tchoutacabouffa River, just north of Biloxi.

**Photograph** courtesy George Ohr Museum

# WILLIAM EGGLESTON
## PHOTOGRAPHER

**"I like to photograph democratically."**

*William Eggleston*

William Eggleston, a figure instrumental in giving legitimacy to color photography as an artistic medium, was raised in Sumner, Mississippi. During his time at both Delta State University and the University of Mississippi, Eggleston developed an interest in photography, and began experimenting with color shortly after. His first exhibition at the Museum of Modern Art, entitled *14 Pictures*, was the first one-person color photography exhibition ever shown at MoMA. This event marked the beginning of color photography as a valid art form. Ingrid Sischy of *Art Forum* remarks, "Eggleston is from and lives in the South, which is, to borrow a term from nuclear physics, the strong force that binds and centers his compositions."

**Photograph** by Maude Schuyler Clay

# WALTER ANDERSON

**"Dogs, cats and birds are holes in heaven through which many will pass."**

*Walter Anderson*

Walter Anderson felt that an artist should create affordable work that brought pleasure to others, and in return, the artist should be able to pursue his artistic passions.

In the late 1930s, Anderson first succumbed to mental illness. His recuperation in the pastoral tranquility of an old plantation provided an ideal setting for Anderson's art. He rendered thousands of disciplined and compelling works.

In 1947, with the understanding of his family, Anderson left his wife and children and embarked on a private and very solitary existence. He lived alone in a cottage on the Shearwater compound. He would row 12 miles in a small skiff to Horn Island, carrying minimal necessities and his art supplies.

Anderson's obsession to "realize" his subjects through his art, to be one with the natural world instead of being an intruder, created works that are intense and evocative.

**Illustration** self portrait by Walter Anderson

# JERE ALLEN

PAINTER

**"My paintings employ a reactive method in the search for an elusive notion that has perplexed me for many years."**
*Jere Allen*

Painter Jere Allen creates bold, intense figurative studies, richly textured suggestions of myth and symbol, and portrayals of "political and social realities." He generates drama through deep contrast: in "Inspirations," Allen interrupts negative space with explosions of dark color, while in "Visit," slivers of light emerge both strained and victorious.

Called "the Mississippi Rembrandt," Allen is a contemporary master of the figurative use of color in painting. His style is an amalgam of Surrealism, Classicism, and Expressionism: a symmetrical perfection of both modern and traditional techniques. While difficult to categorize, his paintings taunt us with what is deeply familiar.

Allen was inspired by the art of his grandmother Annie Bell Rives, whose landscapes and depictions of wild animals spoke deeply to him as a child. The images of animals juxtaposed against the human form, is a constant motif in Allen's work.

During his 28-year tenure with the University of Mississippi's Art Department, Allen gained an international reputation as a figurative artist. His work has been displayed in many galleries and institutions, including the Coos Art Museum in Oregon, the Stadtsche Gallery Paderborn in Germany, and National Academy of Sciences in Washington, D.C.

Allen lives and paints in Oxford, Mississippi.

**Photograph** by Ed Croom • **Story** by Louis Bourgeois

# GLENNRAY TUTOR

PAINTER

**"I want to emphasize that flawless technique alone will never generate a work of art. A perfectly played sonata, without an engaging melody, will fail."**

*Glennray Tutor*

"The paintings of Tutor are like life after a glaucoma operation: A whole new vision is given to us," said legendary writer Barry Hannah of his friend and colleague, painter Glennray Tutor. Tutor's hyper-realistic paintings grace the covers of Hannah's best novels and story collections, a perfect merging of two artists' visions. Tutor's works dazzle the eye, heightening the significance of ordinary objects like comic books and marbles, rendering them glowing specters of our most lucid dreams or haziest childhood memories. Somehow Tutor's vision of what one might find in a back yard, toy box, or kitchen counter takes us into another universe where the mundane becomes ethereal.

A significant painter of the post-World War II generation, Tutor moved to Oxford to study at the University of Mississippi, where he received both bachelor's and master's degrees in art. His early works depict mostly barren landscapes painted in deeply layered colors. During this early phase, he illlustrated books by Michael Bishop and James Tiptree, Jr.

In the early 1980s, Tutor gravitated toward painting in the style that would become known as Photorealism. Having no knowledge at the time of other artists working with this style of painting, Tutor's work in Photorealism was a drastic departure from his previous paintings, trading in desolate images resembling the American Southwest for nostalgic yet unsentimental still life paintings of commonplace artifacts. His trademark impeccable lines and lustrous depth are the byproducts of an almost tortuous work discipline. Spending up to 16 hours a day in the studio, it is Tutor's arduous attention to detail that allows for a row of mason jars to become a glistening, triumphant transcendence: at once pedestrian and otherworldly, as if he paints the details we don't or can't see.

Glennray Tutor's reputation is international, his works having been displayed alongside the likes of Andy Warhol, Roy Lichtenstein, and Robert Rauschenberg. Featured in public, private, and corporate collections around the world, Tutor's art has graced the Cole Pratt Gallery in New Orleans, Rarity Gallery in Greece, Plus One Gallery in London, The International Monetary Fund in Washington, D.C., Frank Marino Gallery in New York City, Mendenhall Gallery in Los Angeles, Seymour Lawrence Collection of American Art, the Roger Horchow Collection of Art, FedEx Corporation, Universal Studios, Nike, Inc., NBC Network, and many others.

Tutor lives and paints in Oxford, Mississippi.

**Photograph** by Marion Tutor • **Story** by Louis Bourgeois

# WILLIAM DUNLAP
## PAINTER

**"Art. . .I don't pretend to understand it. I'm just a slave to it."**
*Bill Dunlap*

The American landscape, its flora and fauna are essential elements in the work of William Dunlap. That and certain iconic Old Masters such as Rembrandt's series of self-portraits that Dunlap quotes in paintings and constructions. He calls what he does hypothetical realism. "The places I paint aren't real, but they could be."

Born in Webster County, Mississippi, Dunlap earned degrees from Mississippi College and the University of Mississippi. His paintings often include the stately Starnes House in Mathiston, Mississippi, and his grandfather's foxhounds as symbols for people seldom seen.

In a career spanning more than four decades, Dunlap has exhibited internationally and is included in numerous public and private collections. He has received awards and honors from the Danforth, Rockefeller, Lila Wallace and Warhol Foundations, as well as the Mississippi Institute of Arts and Letters and the Mississippi Governor's Award for Excellence in the Arts.

*Dunlap*, a 2006 University Press of Mississippi publication with essays by Rick Gruber and Julia Reed, remains a definitive book of the artist's work.

William Dunlap maintains studios in Coral Gables, Florida; McLean, Virginia, and Mathiston, Mississippi

The photograph of Dunlap (right) was commissioned for a *Washingtonian* magazine article on artists and their influences. Dunlap says that Rembrandt is to painters what William Faulkner is to writers — "an intimidating inspiration." Both artists were the same age when their respective likenesses were struck.

**Photograph** Bill Dunlap with Rembrandt self-portrait
Photo by Ron Aira • Story by Louis Bourgeois

# BILL BECKWITH

### SCULPTOR

**"My fascination with the figure, particularly the head, grows each day. I find the challenge of imparting a little life into the clay never-ending."**
*Bill Beckwith*

A bronze likeness of Oxford, Mississippi's most famous son sits cross-legged, smoking a pipe, looking over the town he introduced to American literary consciousness. Sculptor William Beckwith's famous sculpture of a middle-aged William Faulkner is just one example of the many Mississippi icons whose likeness he's cast in bronze.

During his 30-year career, the Greenville native has produced bronze sculptures of Jefferson Davis, soldiers of the 11th Mississippi Infantry, B.B King, Jim Henson, Chucky Mullins, and Chickasaw Chief Piomingo. He now works out of his studio in Taylor, Mississippi, not far down the road from where William Faulkner sits forever in front of City Hall. When not working in his studio, he teaches art at the University of Mississippi.

Beckwith was taught by Leon Koury who was taught by Malvina Hoffman, a long-time student of the great Auguste Rodin.

**Photograph** by Todd Nichols • **Story** by Louis Bourgeois

# MARSHALL & JASON BOULDIN
PORTRAIT ARTISTS

Painter Marshall Bouldin's studio was never off-limits to his children: "Dad encouraged us to be around the studio; he never barred us from coming in," said Jason Bouldin. By inviting Jason to share his creative space, Marshall nurtured a father-son relationship of shared passion for painting, hallmarked by mutual respect, common interest in subject and form, and honest criticism of each other's work. Acclaimed portrait artists, the Bouldins are Mississippi natives and lifelong residents.

Octogenarian Marshall, who lives in Clarksdale, was declared "the south's foremost portrait artist" by *The New York Times* and has painted over 800 portraits of politicians, business leaders, and private citizens of considerable note. The first artist to be inducted into the National Portrait Hall of Fame, his work hangs in the White House and the U.S. Capitol. In June of 2009, he received a Lifetime Achievement Award from the Mississippi Institute of Arts and Letters.

Jason Bouldin, of Oxford, was named one of the "20 Contemporary Artists on the Rise" by *The Artist's Magazine*. Painting professionally since 1991, he received first place for portraiture in *The Artist's Magazine*'s 16th annual art competition in 1999 and the Portrait Society of America's grand prize in 2002.

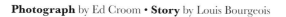

**Photograph** by Ed Croom • **Story** by Louis Bourgeois

# RICHMOND BARTHÉ

SCULPTOR

**"Aesthetically, he brought a new insight to the individuality and physical grace of all types of black people."**

*Romare Bearden*

Pioneering sculptor Richmond Barthé synthesized the collective African-American experience through his work as an artist. His sculptures expressed a range of experiences, depicting African-Americans as workers, warriors, and victims of racial violence. These powerful thematic portrayals, among the first created by an African-American artist, gave dignity to degradation.

The master artist was born in 1901 in Bay St. Louis, Mississippi. His widowed seamstress mother provided the young Barthé with pencil and paper to keep him busy while she worked. Barthé quickly revealed himself as a natural artist: the gift of a watercolor set made him a painter at age six. By his teenage years, Barthé's paintings began to attract the attention of the Bay St. Louis community.

An admirer arranged for him to take a job with a prominent New Orleans family, wealthy patrons of the arts. It was while working as a houseboy that Barthé became a part of the New Orleans artistic community, buoying him from servant to serious artist. There he met writer Lyle Saxon who urged him to pursue art as a career. With no southern art schools willing to accept black students, a Catholic priest paid for Barthé to attend the prestigious Art Institute of Chicago where he was encouraged by teacher Charles Schroeder to try sculpture for the first time. His first bust unveiled a natural talent for the medium.

Within ten years Barthé had built an international reputation as a sculptor. His works remain highly regarded features of the Whitney Museum of American Art, the Metropolitan Museum of Art, and the Smithsonian Institution.

Barthé died in Pasadena, California, in 1989.

**Photograph**: Richmond Barthé with his sculpture Mask of a Boy, circa 1931
Courtesy of Richmond Barthé Papers, Amistad Research Center at Tulane University, New Orleans, Louisiana
**Story** by Louis Bourgeois

# MAUDE SCHUYLER CLAY

PHOTOGRAPHER

Mississippi photographer Maude Schuyler Clay's black and white images of Delta landscapes brim with cotton fields, shacks, swamps, and old dogs. Her classic images suggest an eerie, quiet rumbling beneath the surface stillness, giving the impression of a world that cannot or will not be touched by time.

Born in Greenwood, Mississippi, Schuyler attended the University of Mississippi and the Memphis Academy of Arts in the early 1970s. Following in the footsteps of her photographer cousin William Eggleston, her 1999 collection of photography, *Delta Land*, was an instant commercial and critical success.

Former photo editor for *The Oxford American*, Clay's work has appeared in *Vanity Fair*, *Esquire*, and *The New York Times Magazine*. In 2001, one of her "Delta Dogs" photographs graced the cover of the late Barry Hannah's last novel, *Yonder Stands Your Orphan*. Clay's photographs are permanently housed in The Museum of Modern Art, the Museum of Fine Arts in Houston, and the National Museum for Women in the Arts in Washington, D.C.

She resides with her family in Sumner, Mississippi.

**Photograph** by Jerry Siegel • **Story** by Louis Bourgeois

# LANGDON CLAY

PHOTOGRAPHER

Langdon Clay was born in New York City and raised in New England.

He photographs around the country and beyond for shelter magazines and coffee table books. The bulk of his commercial work involves architecture, interiors, gardens and food. His work is featured in *Jefferson's Monticello* by Howard Adams and *From My Chateau Kitchen* by Anne Willan. His art photography can be found in museums in Paris, London, New York, Chicago, New Orleans and Jackson, Mississippi.

He resides on the banks of Cassidy Bayou in the little delta town of Sumner with his wife, photographer Maude Schuyler Clay, and three children: Anna, Schuyler, and Sophie.

**Photograph** by Langdon Clay

# BIRNEY IMES

PHOTOGRAPHER, PUBLISHER

**"I saw that photograph of the men standing around the pool table and read that phrase
'2-kool 2-be 4-gotten,' and the inspiration was obvious. Every time I sing that song, I credit Birney Imes.
Birney's work is, in photography, what a good blues song is to me — gritty, edgy in all its parallels."**

*Lucinda Williams*

For more than 20 years Birney Imes roamed the countryside of his native Mississippi photographing the people and places he encountered along the way. Working in both black and white and color, Imes' photographs take viewers inside juke joints and dilapidated restaurants scattered across that landscape. There he introduces the viewer to, as one writer put it, "the characters and locales that linger in the margins of Southern memory and culture."

Imes' photographs have been collected in three books: *Juke Joint*, *Whispering Pines*, and *Partial to Home*, and have been exhibited in solo shows in the United States and Europe. His work is included in the collections of the Museum of Modern Art and the Metropolitan Museum of Art in New York, The Art Institute of Chicago, The Bibliotheque Nationale in Paris and numerous public and private collections in the U.S. and abroad.

In 1996, with the illness of his father, Imes began working at *The* (Columbus, Mississippi) *Commercial Dispatch*, the daily newspaper that has been in his family for four generations.

**Photograph** by Jerry Siegel

# JOHN DAVIS

ARTIST

Water Valley artist John Davis is an artisan in every sense of the word. He's the kind they don't make much any more. He begins the creative process by walking into the woods. He lies on the ground and stares up at the trees. He looks for inspiration . . . and the perfectly shaped branch with which to begin his work.

Davis' works include chairs, tables, bowls, combs, bangos, bows (as in bows and arrows) and grandfather clocks. When you encounter Davis and his work, you can count on two things: great conversation and a one-of-a-kind creation.

**Photograph** by Todd Nichols

243

# DAVID RAE MORRIS
PHOTOGRAPHER

David Rae Morris was born in Oxford, England and grew up in New York City. He had an early interest in photography and attended night classes at the International Center of Photography. He received a B.A. from Hampshire College in Amherst, MA, in 1982, and an M.A. in Journalism and Mass Communication from the University of Minnesota in 1991. His photographs have been published in *Time Magazine*, *Newsweek*, *USA Today*, *New York Times*, *Utne Reader*, *The Nation*, and the *Angolite*, the official Magazine of the Louisiana State Penitentiary at Angola. He has also served as a contributing photographer for the Associated Press, Reuters, the European Pressphoto Agency, and Polaris Images.

In 1999, Morris collaborated with his late father, the noted author Willie Morris, on *My Mississippi*, a collection of essays and photographs about the state of Mississippi and her people published by the University Press of Mississippi. His photographs are in many private and public collections including the permanent collections of the Ogden Museum of Southern Art, the Louisiana State Museum in New Orleans, and the Mississippi Museum of Art in Jackson. His exhibit, "Do You Know What it Means? The Aftermath of Hurricane Katrina," opened at the Ogden Museum of Southern Art ten weeks after Katrina made landfall. His post-Katrina work has also been featured in numerous journals and magazines and in the book, *Missing New Orleans*, published by the Ogden in November 2005.

Four of his photographs were used in the introductory credits for the HBO series, "Treme."

**Photograph** shadow in New Orleans muck post-Katrina. Self-portrait by David Rae Morris

# STEPHEN KIRKPATRICK

PHOTOGRAPHER

Stephen Kirkpatrick's stunning nature photography reveals an intimate glimpse into the mysterious and beautiful world of Mississippi flora and fauna. His photographs invite the viewer to tip-toe stealthily and quietly into Mississippi's woodlands, wetlands, and prairies to see the abundant wildlife the state offers.

Having published over 3,000 wildlife photographs in books and magazines worldwide, some of his most well known books of photography include *Wild Mississippi*, *Mississippi Impressions*, *Among the Animals: Mississippi*, and *Whistling Wings: The Beauty of Ducks in Flight*. He is also the winner of the 2002 National Outdoor Book Award and the Southeastern Outdoor Press Association's 2002 Book of the Year.

He resides in Madison, Mississippi, with his wife and photography partner, Marlo Carter Kirkpatrick.

**Photograph** courtesy Stephen Kirkpatrick

# JANE RULE BURDINE
PHOTOGRAPHER

A native of Greenville and a Deltan to her core, Jane Rule Burdine nonetheless migrated to the hills of Lafayette County in 1984 and bought an old farm house in Taylor, Mississippi, seven miles south of Oxford. Her photographer's focus remained on her beloved flat land, culminating in a 2008 book, *Delta Deep Down* (University Press of Mississippi). Prior to this, her lens explored the devastating poverty of the pre-casino Sugar Ditch area near Tunica. In between, she spent years prowling the back roads of Mississippi — Hot Coffee to Alligator — absorbing the landscapes and bonding with her subjects.

Jane Rule also served as mayor of Taylor, Mississippi for 12 years, where she could often be spotted patrolling the little village in a golf cart. She is a veteran cat lover, avid flower gardener, gourmet cook, and hostess of spontaneous late night dinners. She is also known as a discerning collector of southern esoterica. From her two small warehouses, she could outfit a small town in dresses, vintage furnishings, and retro furniture. In her work and in her sensibilities, Jane Rule Burdine brings life to art and vice versa.

# MILDRED NUNGESTER WOLFE

PAINTER

**"I get excited about everyday accidents of atmosphere and light. Every painting is an attempt to remember and make a permanent record of a moment of intense visual perception: the delicate arabesque of weeds silhouetted against the deep russet of sedge, a sharp blue sky, the unbelievable grace of birds, etched on my memory."**

*Mildred Nungester Wolfe*

In 1988, one of the most prominent artists from Mississippi, Mildred Nungester Wolfe, expertly painted one of the most well-known writers from Mississippi. This iconic portrait of Eudora Welty now hangs in the National Portrait Gallery in Washington, D.C. A blend of Impressionism and Post-Impressionism, Wolfe's art can be seen across Mississippi, from the Mississippi Museum of Art to the Methodist Children's Home in Jackson. Shortly after Eudora Welty's portrait was completed, Wolfe and Welty teamed up to write and illustrate a book titled *Morgana: Two Stories from "The Golden Apples."*

**Photograph** courtesy Bebe Wolfe

# LEE & PUP MCCARTY

POTTERS

**"We had a choice: the Cranbrook Academy of Art in California, or back home. We chose home."**

*Lee McCarty*

McCarty pottery is world famous. And it began with William Faulkner pointing out a clay deposit on his property and telling Lee and Pup McCarty that they could have it. Today, the McCartys' work is displayed in museums and galleries around the world. Focusing on both artistic and functional pieces, the McCartys' creations fill homes and galleries with dinnerware, hanging planters, lamps, platters and sculptures. In 1991, the Samuel P. Harn Museum of Art at the University of Florida in Gainesville held a retrospective called "Mud Magic: the Mississippi Pottery of Lee & Pup McCarty." In 1997, they received a Lifetime Achievement Award from the Mississippi Institute of Arts and Letters.

**Photograph** courtesy McCarty Pottery

# HYSTERCINE RANKIN

QUILTER

Once she began quilting at age 12, Lorman native Hystercine Rankin never stopped. Her unique style of memory quilts and embellished traditional quilts are her signature, one that she has shared with students at Mississippi Cultural Crossroads, as well as members of the Crossroads Quilters. She won the Susan B. Herron Fellowship from the Mississippi Arts Commission in 1991 and served as a demonstrator at the 1996 Festival of American Folklife in Washington, D.C. In 1997 she received a National Heritage Fellowship from the National Endowment for the Arts.

**Photograph** by Beth Batton

# SAMUEL MARSHALL GORE

PAINTER, SCULPTOR, TEACHER

**"As a teacher, I share what I can demonstrate in actual performance. I am still learning."**

*Samuel Marshall Gore*

The art program at Mississippi College might not exist if it weren't for Samuel Marshall Gore. He was a part of the faculty for 60 years, and took the program from having one professor to six, created the curriculum for art majors and created the Sam Gore Art Scholarship Endowment. Under his leadership Mississippi College hosted the first loan exhibit in the South from the Guggenheim Museum. MC was the first of 40 Southern Baptist Colleges to offer an MFA degree program. And the school was the first among the small colleges to have a graduate elected to membership in the National Sculpture Society.

As an artist, Gore has both painted and sculpted, focusing on sculpting in more recent years.

**Photograph** courtesy Mississippi College

# LEON Z. KOURY
SCULPTOR

Leon Koury was born in Greenville in 1909 to Syrian immigrants. Early in his life, Koury wanted to become a writer or poet. After local poet William Alexander Percy, from whom Koury hoped to receive advice on writing, saw the drawing's on Koury's notebook, Percy encouraged Koury to pursue art — sculpture in particular. Not only did he become one of the most talented and acclaimed sculptors of his time, he is also part of one of the most impressive lines of artists and teachers in history. Koury was taught by Malvina Hoffman, a long-time student of the great Auguste Rodin. Koury, in turn, taught William Beckwith — a current Mississippi great — how to sculpt in the tradition of those artists before him. Koury's famous bust of William Alexander Percy was covered by both *Time* and *Life* magazines in 1964.

**Photograph** courtesy Bill Beckwith

# SULTON ROGERS

CARVER

Oxford-born Sulton (also spelled Sultan) Rogers learned carpentry at an early age, but didn't use his skills much until, while working night shifts at a chemical plant in Syracuse, New York, he began carving to keep himself awake. Rogers retired in 1984 and moved back to Mississippi where he began carving full time. His work often depicts naturally rendered bodies with distorted facial expressions, as well as vampires, haints and religious material. His carvings have become permanent fixtures in museums across the United States.

**Photograph** by Milly Moorhead West

# ETHEL WRIGHT MOHAMED

TEXTILE ARTIST

**"Listen, as I pull the needle through the material, it makes music.
I think that's the reason I'm so enchanted with it."**

*Ethel Mohamed*

Sometimes called "Mississippi's Grandma Moses of stitchery," Ethel Wright Mohamed used her needle and thread to create visual stories of her family's life. Born in Fame, Mississippi, her stitchery has achieved international acclaim and can be found in the Smithsonian American Art Museum, among others.

# WYATT WATERS

PAINTER

Wyatt Waters offers a new perspective of Mississippi: a seamless impressionistic expression of the familiar.

In *Another Coat of Paint: An Artist's View of Jackson, Mississippi*, Waters reveals a city to itself, exploring its oddities, remembering its landmarks and inhabitants.

Born in Brookhaven, Mississippi, in 1955, Waters first garnered attention as a painter in the 1980s, painting famous places in and around Jackson. Waters' art has been exhibited at the Meridian Museum of Art, and in Bryant Galleries in both Jackson and New Orleans, as well as many others. His work has been published in *American Artist Magazine*, *Watercolor 87*, and *Mississippi Magazine*. In 2010, Wyatt received the coveted Governor's Award for Excellence in the Arts in Mississippi.

In addition to his painting, Waters has influenced a generation of young artists through his classes at Mississippi College and Millsaps. He has also worked as Artist in Residence in the Clinton and Meridian Public Schools.

He lives and works in Clinton, Mississippi.

**Photograph** courtesy Wyatt Waters

# MILLY MOORHEAD WEST

PHOTOGRAPHER

A photographer in Oxford, Mississippi, Milly Moorhead West has just about done it all. She has worked as a production assistant, still photographer, and camera operator for several locally produced films; she has taught photography, drawing, painting and other classes at universities in Oklahoma and Mississippi; and she was the owner and director of Oxford's Southside Gallery from 1993-2002. Her own photographs have appeared in *Mississippi Magazine*, *Visualizing the Blues*, and *The Oxford American*, among others; her work has also been displayed in galleries across the South. In 1996, she received the Mississippi Institute of Arts and Letters Award in Photography.

**Photograph:** Self portrait by Milly Moorhead West

# MARIE HULL

IMPRESSIONIST

**"Any reference to art in Mississippi and the South since the early part of the 20th century would not be complete without Marie Hull. Her art and life as a painter and teacher have influenced hundreds of young artists to make their way in art."**

*Marion Barnwell*

Lifelong artist Marie Hull was born in Summit, Mississippi, halfway between Jackson and New Orleans. By gleaning culture from these two cities, she learned to appreciate art at a very young age. Although she was interested in music, and studied music at Belhaven College, Marie's true legacy resides in her paintings. At the age of 20, she realized she "wanted to paint more than anything else." She specialized in still-life and abstraction, but was constantly exploring new mediums and techniques. Her work has been exhibited at the Art Institute of Chicago, The Paris Autumn Salon, the New York World's Fair (1939), and the San Francisco Golden Gate Exhibition (1939). Governor William Waller honored her impact on Mississippi art by naming October 22, 1975 Marie Hull Day.

# WILLIAM GOODMAN

## ARTIST

**"Though a young emerging artist, William's work embodies the dark sensuality of the 70s and 80s, and strongly appeals to both those who have lived during those times and those who can only imagine it."**

*Lorna York, Madison Gallery, La Jolla, California*

In the first grade, William Goodman was chastised by his teacher for drawing creatures when he should have been paying attention. At home, he pasted cut-out images on every inch of his bedroom. By the time he was 24 years old, Goodman had his first art exhibit in New York City.

Goodman's work has been shown in galleries in New York, Chicago, Washington DC, Little Rock, New Orleans, and the West Coast. In 2008, his creations were featured in *New American Paintings* — and his works are held in prominent collections across the United States.

Marcy Nessel of Fischer Galleries said, "William Goodman is the most promising young artist Mississippi has seen in some time. He is a rising star whose work is sought after by clients and galleries across the nation."

Goodman's paintings — described by one critic as "raw emotion on the canvas" — mirror modern culture and reflect his fascination with the past. While Goodman is looking back for inspiration, the art world looks forward to more of his work.

**Photograph:** Tom Beck

# ANDREW BUCCI

PAINTER

Andrew Bucci, a native of Vicksburg, is considered one of the greatest of living Mississippi artists. He began studying with Marie Hull in the late 1930s. While serving in the military in WWII, he was able to study painting in Paris and upon his return, he received a BFA and MFA from the Art Institute of Chicago. He continued to study with Marie Hull and the two influenced one another in their respective work. He relocated to Maryland in the late 50s, where he continues to paint today. In 1967 he designed the United States Postal Service stamp for the 150th anniversary of Mississippi statehood. In 2009 he received the Lifetime Achievement award from the Mississippi Governor's Award for the Arts.

# MARTIN HODGES

## SCULPTOR

He begins with a sheet of metal. As he hammers the cold steel — without the benefit of molds — human form takes shape. Martin Hodges started out as a kid who wanted to make his own armor. The idea of a second skin intrigued him. For years he toiled and hammered, perfecting his technique. Then, he decided to try something new — making a piece of armor for a female.

It was meant to be a one-time project. But now Hodges' female nudes are in high demand. One of the few artists working in cold metal (he says his technique falls somewhere between silver-smithing and armoring), Hodges' work is getting attention from galleries and collectors throughout the South.

In a remote cabin in Sunflower County, working with nothing more than a few hammers, a railroad spike, and his great uncle's anvil from the early 1900s, Hodges is creating one-of-a-kind nudes so real you'll believe he peeled a second skin of metal from a human torso.

**Photograph** courtesy Andrew's Forge

INNOVATORS & VISIONARIES

# REUBEN ANDERSON
## ATTORNEY, TRAILBLAZER

Reuben Anderson has broken more legal barriers than any other Mississippian. Anderson, a Jackson native, was the first African-American graduate of the University of Mississippi School of Law. In 1981, Governor William Winter appointed Anderson to the Circuit Court bench (the first black Circuit Court Judge since Reconstruction). In 1985, Governor Bill Allain appointed him to the Mississippi State Supreme Court. He was twice re-elected to the high court (where he served as Presiding Judge). And in 1996, he was elected as President of the Mississippi Bar Association. All firsts for Mississippi.

Anderson is a partner at Phelps Dunbar, LLC. He serves on the Board of Directors of AT&T and The Kroger Company.

**Photograph** courtesy The University of Mississippi

# ROBERT KHAYAT
### EDUCATOR, ATHLETE, VISIONARY

Robert Khayat made Mississippi a better place to live, work and learn — and in the process, a nation changed the way it viewed our state. As an Academic All-American football and baseball player, an All-Pro NFL athlete, and holder of degrees from Ole Miss and Yale, Khayat could have accepted lucrative positions in private enterprise. Instead, he chose the path of education and service.

As the 15th Chancellor of the University of Mississippi, Khayat, a Moss Point native, led the school through a renaissance. On four campuses, enrollment increased to more than 17,000. Faculty and staff compensation increased (Ole Miss was ranked in the top 10 places to work in higher education). Private support soared. And innovative programs like the Sally McDonnell Barksdale Honors College, the Croft Institute for International Studies, and the Trent Lott Leadership Institute pumped new life into the University.

Under Khayat's leadership, Ole Miss was selected to shelter a chapter of Phi Beta Kappa, and the school was listed among the nation's Top 25 public universities. And in 2008 all eyes were on the university as it hosted the first of four presidential debates between Barack Obama and John McCain.

In 2011, the new building for the University's law school was named in his honor: The Robert C. Khayat Law Center.

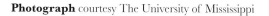

**Photograph** courtesy The University of Mississippi

# ARTHUR C. GUYTON, M.D.

PHYSIOLOGIST

**"Physiology is indeed an explanation of life. What other subject matter is more fascinating, more exciting, more beautiful than the subject of life."**

*Arthur C. Guyton*

Arthur Clifton Guyton was a physiologist born in Oxford, Mississippi to a doctor and a physics teacher. Guyton's *Textbook of Medical Physiology*, which includes nine editions (eight of which were written solely by Guyton), continues to be studied in nearly every medical school in the country. Guyton had intended to be a surgeon, but a case of polio rendered him partially paralyzed, so he chose to improve the medical world in other ways. While struggling with his physical state after recovering from polio, Guyton invented a number of innovative devices, including the very first motorized wheelchair controlled by a joystick, and special leg braces. For these inventions he received a Presidential Citation.

After Guyton's recovery, he returned to Oxford where he devoted himself to teaching and research at the University of Mississippi School of Medicine and was named chair of the department of Physiology in 1948. In 1951 he was named one of the 10 outstanding men in the nation. When the University of Mississippi moved its Medical School to Jackson in 1955, he rapidly developed one of the world's premier cardiovascular research programs.

Upon his death in 2003, Guyton left behind 10 children, all of whom became noted physicians themselves.

**Photograph** courtesy University of Mississippi Medical Center

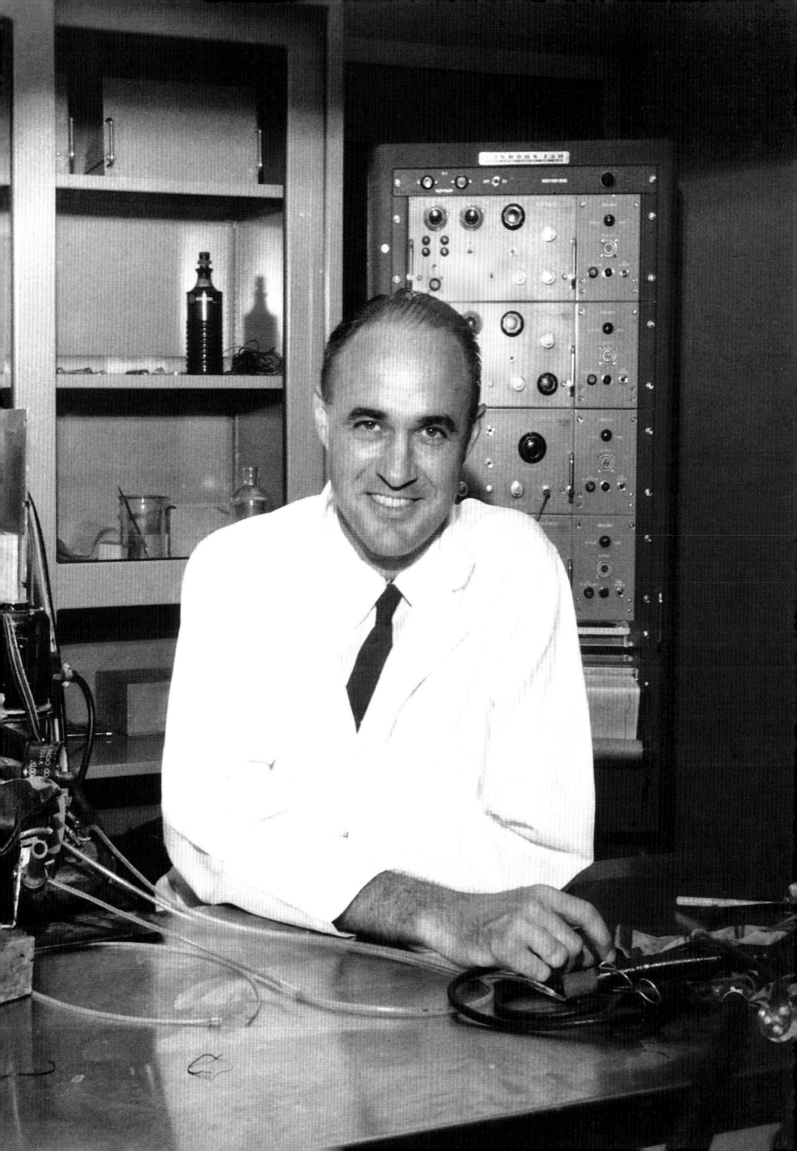

# JAMES HARDY, M.D.

SURGEON

Beginning in 1955, James Hardy served as the Chair of Surgery and the first ever Professor of Surgery at the University of Mississippi School of Medicine. Hardy performed the world's first successful human lung transplant in 1963. He also performed the first successful animal-to-human heart transplant. In 1987, Hardy led the team that performed a double-lung transplant that left the heart in place.

On the evening of the first human lung transplant operation, Medgar Evers died in the same hospital's emergency room. Dr. Hardy's chief resident, Dr. Martin Dalton, left the operating room in an attempt to save Mr. Evers' life. When Dr. Hardy emerged from having successfully completed this climax to years of laboratory effort, he found that the clamor outside the operating room suite was not about the world's first lung transplant but about the horrific assasination.

The following day, news of the lung transplant went virtually unnoticed.

Hardy produced 24 books,139 book chapters, 466 papers, and over 200 films. He held 36 visiting professorships during his career, and he served as the president of several surgical associations, including the International Society of Surgery and the American Surgical Association.

Hardy died on February 19, 2003, at the age of 84.

**Photograph** courtesy University of Mississippi Medical Center

# SAMBO MOCKBEE

ARCHITECT

**"Physical poverty is not an abstraction, but we almost never think of impoverishment as evidence of a world that exists. Much less do we imagine that it's a condition from which we may draw enlightenment in a very practical way."**

*Sambo Mockbee*

A visionary architect from Meridian, Mississippi, Samuel "Sambo" Mockbee was the co-founder of the Auburn University Rural Studio program. In 1993, he receieved a grant from the Graham Foundation for Advanced Studies in the Fine Arts to work toward publishing his book, *The Nurturing of Culture in the Rural South: An Architectonic Documentary.* He also received a MacArthur Foundation Genius Grant. Part architect, part activist, part sage, Mockbee believed that "everyone, rich or poor, deserved a shelter for the soul."

In 1998 Mockee was diagnosed with leukemia and fought toward a recovery, but suffered a relapse three years later and passed away in 2001. In 2004, he posthumously received a Gold Medal from the American Institute of Architects.

**Photograph** by Maude Schuyler Clay

# ZIG ZIGLAR
MOTIVATIONAL SPEAKER

**"When you're tough on yourself, life is going to be infinitely easier on you."**

*Zig Ziglar*

When Zig Ziglar was five years old, his father accepted a management position at a Mississippi farm, and his family moved to Yazoo City, where he spent most of his early childhood. Ziglar worked a variety of sales jobs as a young man, during which time his sales skills improved and his interest in motivational speaking grew. Ziglar went into the business of motivational speaking full-time in 1970. Since then, he has trained thousands in the art of positive thinking and success strategies.

Ziglar's books include *Zig Ziglar's Secrets of Closing the Sale*, *Top Performance: How to Develop Excellence in Yourself and Others*, *See You at the Top*, and *Embrace The Struggle*.

Dave Ramsey called Ziglar "a National Treasure."

**Photograph** by Getty Images

# WILLIAM FERRIS

SCHOLAR, FOLKLORIST, ENDOWMENT FOR THE HUMANITIES CHAIR

**"Bill Ferris leads the sort of life I'd like to lead if I had another one to live."**
*President Bill Clinton*

Perhaps no one has influenced the world's view of the modern South more than William Ferris. Ferris' fieldwork as a folklorist began on his family's Vicksburg farm. Mules, blues musicians, horse traders, storytellers, African-American gospel singing in the small church whose congregation sang their hymns from memory — all fascinated the young Ferris.

He studied under the renowned folklorist, Kenneth Goldstein. Ferris was the first native Mississippian to study and document African-American folk culture in the state and assign it an important place in American studies scholarship. After teaching two years as a professor at Jackson State University and a seven-year stint teaching American and African-American studies at Yale, in 1979 Ferris became the first director of the newly-established Center for the Study of Southern Culture at the University of Mississippi. Presenting the rich and protean culture of the South as a solid academic discipline, Ferris and Ole Miss began to attract graduate students from the nation's finest universities. He brought Alice Walker, Alex Haley, Toni Morrison, and Margaret Walker Alexander to Oxford. And with Ferris' encouragement, B.B. King donated his extensive record collection to launch the Blues Archives at Ole Miss.

Through Bill Ferris' interpretation of the South, it became recognized as somehow more interesting, its culture more rich, its people more creative and intelligent. More than anyone else, Bill Ferris made the South something it had never been. Bill Ferris made the South cool.

**Photograph** by Lucian Perkins/The Washington Post

# FRED HAISE

ASTRONAUT

Biloxi native Fred Haise is one of only 24 people to have flown to the Moon. He was selected as a NASA astronaut in 1966 and was the first of his group to be assigned to Apollo duties. Haise was the lunar module pilot on the aborted Apollo 13 lunar mission in 1970. Due to the free return trajectory on that mission, Haise probably shares the record for the furthest distance from the Earth ever traveled by human beings. Haise later flew five flights as the commander of the space shuttle Enterprise.

Haise was presented with the Presidential Medal of Freedom in 1970 by President Richard Nixon. Bill Paxton played the role of Haise in the film *Apollo 13*.

**Photograph** courtesy Keystone, Hulton Archive

# ROD PAIGE

**"I have been fortunate to devote my entire professional life to education. I meant it from the bottom of my heart when I said no child should be left behind."**

*Rod Paige*

Rod Paige, born in Monticello, Mississippi, served under President George W. Bush as the seventh United States Secretary of Education. A graduate of Jackson State University, Paige was the first African-American to serve as Secretary of Education. He is the Chairman of the Chartwell Education Group, he created the PEER program, and is a member of the NAACP. From 1964 to 1968, before pursuing a political career, Paige was the head football coach for Jackson State University.

**Photograph** by Mark Wilson, Getty Images News

# JOHN CURRENCE

RESTAURATEUR, CHEF

**"I think it is a true testament to John's talent and to him as a person to see what an impact he's made on the food world from a town of just about 10,000 people."**

*Kelly English, chef/owner of Restaurant Iris in Memphis*

Since 1992, entrepreneurial chef John Currence has garnered international attention for his innovative culinary creations in the small town of Oxford, Mississippi. From his early re-invention of shrimp and grits (still one of the top draws for Oxford visitors) to his ingredient-driven Big Bad Breakfast menu honoring the town's literary heritage, Currence continues to push himself toward loftier aspirations.

After winning the New Orleans 2008 Great American Seafood Cookoff and the 2009 James Beard Award for Best Chef: South, Currence competed in season 3 of *Top Chef Masters*. Though he didn't win the whole competition, his participation earned some funds for No Kid Hungry, a charity dedicated to eradicating childhood hunger in the United States. His City Grocery Restaurant Group now operates four outstanding eateries (City Grocery, Bouré, Big Bad Breakfast, and Snackbar); he contributed to 2010's *Wild Abundance: Ritual, Revelry & Recipes of the South's Finest Hunting Clubs*; he serves as contributing editor to *Garden & Gun* magazine; and he's back in Oxford and busy as ever, opening a new location on the Square for his Creole-infused restaurant, Bouré.

**Photograph** by Bruce Newman

# GEORGE SCHLOEGEL

### MAYOR

By a landslide, Gulfport native George Schloegel won the 2009 mayoral election in Mississippi's second largest city. Not unusual, except that he was 69 years old.

Schloegel's list of accomplishments in the private sector are impressive. He served as president and CEO of Hancock Bank (he started as a 16-year-old mailroom employee); he was a founding father of Leadership Mississippi; and for decades he served as a mentor to young bankers across the South.

Now, Schloegel is bringing his innovation and creativity to the public sector, reinventing the way city government operates — from public/private partnerships to cleaning up dilapidated properties. He instituted a green program so citizens can sponsor "memory trees" to honor loved ones (the trees will be planted along Gulfport's boulevards and parks). He's been imaginative in reducing budget deficits without curtailing vital services. And he's really thinking outside the box on education. Last year, the first public, free pre-school in south Mississippi was launched in the city of Gulfport. In the pilot program, 22 students (all four-year-olds) graduated, and based on pre- and post-testing, the students mastered a full year's curriculum in just 88 days. Keep an eye on the city of Gulfport — and its mayor. Both could be new models.

**Photograph** Gulfport Mayor George Schloegel (left) and Mississippi Gov. Haley Barbour (right) visit with President Obama following a roundtable discussion with local residents about tourism post-BP oil spill. Photo by Mandel Ngan/AFP

# JACK REED

VISIONARY, ORATOR, MERCHANT

**"We must support public education and keep our schools open."**

*Jack Reed, in a 1963 speech to the
Mississippi Economic Council*

For more than five decades, Jack Reed has been a voice of reason. Hardly one to follow the status quo, Reed, a Tupelo native, spoke from the position of a prominent businessman, as well as a leader in education, race relations, and economic development. A great orator, Reed delivered speeches with great cheer. But they weren't always received in that manner — especially in the 1960s when he spoke on behalf of public education and racial equality.

Pulitzer Prize-winning journalist William Raspberry noted, "Jack Reed was brave when it counted." Former Mississippi Governor William Winter wrote, "No person in my lifetime has done more to inspire and try to lead our state in the way it should go than Jack Reed."

*A Time to Speak*, a collection of Reed's speeches delivered over a 50-year period, was published in 2009. Recently, he was honored by the Boys & Girls Clubs of North Mississippi as the 2011 Champion for Youth.

**Photograph** by Steve Jones

# RAY MABUS

STATESMAN

Ray Mabus, a Harvard Law graduate and protégé of William Winter, was elected Mississippi State Auditor in 1983. During his tenure, Mabus' "Operation Pretense" ensnared 57 county supervisors in 25 counties for misuse of public funds. Mabus fundamentally changed how county government functioned in the state by raising the profile of the State Auditor's office.

Mabus was subsequently elected as the 60th Governor of Mississippi. During his time as governor, he passed one of the most comprehensive education reform programs in America, gave teachers the largest pay raise in the nation, and was named one of *Fortune Magazine*'s "education governors."

Mabus also served as U.S. Ambassador to Saudi Arabia. He is the current U.S. Secretary of the Navy.

**Photograph** Ray Mabus (right) is sworn in as the 75th Secretary of the Navy. Photo courtesy U.S. Navy

# RICHARD HOWORTH
BOOKSELLER

Richard Howorth has had an immeasurable impact on the town of Oxford, Mississippi. From opening his independent bookstore, Square Books, in 1979, to serving as the city's mayor from 2001 to 2009, Howorth has affected the town economically, culturally, and politically. A supporter of the indoor smoking ban, bicycle-friendly streets, and a public bus system, Howorth helped to move Oxford a little further into the 21st century without sacrificing the town's charm.

Faulkner's Rowan Oak and Howorth's Square Books make an unbeatable combination. The two have made Oxford *the* literary destination of the South.

As president of the American Bookseller Association, Howorth led the campaign against Barnes & Noble's purchase of Ingram (a fight the independent bookstores won). He also oversaw the creation of Book Sense and BookSense.com.

Recently, Howorth was nominated by President Obama, and later approved by the Senate, for a position on the Tennessee Valley Authority Board of Directors, and has spoken about his goals for utilizing greener electricity methods.

**Photograph** Richard Howorth (center) with Barry Hannah and Willie Morris circa 1984. Photo by Milly Moorhead West

# JOE BIEDENHARN

BOTTLING AND AVIATION INNOVATOR

After the Civil War, Joe Biedenharn was working in the Vicksburg family business, Biedenharn and Sons Candy Company, when a salesman from Atlanta brought him an item to sell in the store. It was called Coca-Cola. It was sold as an over-the-counter carbonated drink. Biedenharn grew tired of waiting on suppliers to bring him carbonated water so he bought a used machine and started bottling his own flavored carbonated water. One day, he got the bright idea of mixing in the Coca-Cola syrup. It was the first time Coca-Cola was bottled — and that began the Coca-Cola Bottling Company.

Later, Biedenharn and his sons were the major backers of a crop-dusting industry, which turned into Delta Airlines.

**Photograph** courtesy of Biedenharn Museum

# ELIZABETH LEE HAZEN

SCIENTIST

Orphaned at the age of three and raised by relatives in Rich, Mississippi, Elizabeth Lee Hazen was a pioneer in biology and chemistry. She developed nystatin, the first non-toxic drug for treating human fungal infections. The drug cured many disfiguring and disabling fungal infections of the mouth, skin, throat, and intestinal tract.

A graduate of the Mississippi University for Women, she taught biology and physics in Jackson until she was accepted into Columbia University for graduate studies. She received her Ph.D. in 1927 as one of Columbia's first female doctoral students. Her research on fungi had multiple uses, from saving human lives to restoring mold-damaged artwork.

**Photograph** courtesy Mississippi University for Women

# DORIS TAYLOR
RESEARCHER

Doris Taylor, a native of Mound Bayou, Mississippi, is making medical history. In 2008, she and her team at the University of Minnesota developed a process called whole-organ decellurization which led to the creation of a completely new, beating heart in the laboratory. Taylor's expertise is in cardiology and stem cells, and she is a Professor of Integrative Biology and Physiology as well as the Director of the Center for Cardiovascular Repair in Minnesota. She hopes that her research and lab work can eventually lead to the creation of new donor organs.

**Photograph** courtesy University of Minnesota

# ANDY MULLINS

EDUCATION VISIONARY

Currently the Chief of Staff to the Chancellor and Associate Professor of Education at the University of Mississippi, Dr. Andy Mullins has made an enormous impact on Mississippi education. After graduating from Millsaps in 1970, Mullins fell in love with teaching. Later, when working as then-Governor William Winter's education advisor, he helped create the 1982 Education Reform Act, which, among other things, put public kindergarten in schools and helped create the alternate route for potential teachers who didn't major in education. In 1989, he co-founded with Amy Gutman the Mississippi Teacher Corps, a program, similar to the Peace Corps intended to fill Mississippi's teacher shortage. Since 1989, the program has provided more than 450 participants with teaching positions in critical-needs school districts.

Mullins has worked as a special assistant to three Chancellors, as an education advisor to two governors and as an advisor to three state superintendents of education. Mullins was instrumental in the founding of the Lott Leadership Institute and the Winter Institute for Racial Reconciliation. He is the co-founder of the Mississippi Principal Corps and he chaired the steering committee that brought the only presidential debate to Mississippi in 2008.

Mullins has dedicated the last 41 years of his life to improving education in Mississippi. He is the first to admit we still have much work to do. But we wouldn't be nearly so far along were it not for Andy Mullins.

**Photograph** courtesy the University of Mississippi

# L.Q.C. LAMAR

SECRETARY OF INTERIOR, SUPREME COURT JUSTICE

Lucius Quintus Cincinnatus Lamar was not born in Mississippi, but once he lived here, he never stayed away for too long. In 1849 he took a teaching position at Ole Miss for one year, and then began practicing law in Oxford. He established his own plantation, which he called Solitude, in the surrounding county. After moving to Georgia for a couple of years, he returned to Mississippi and represented the state in the U.S. House of Representatives and the U.S. Senate. In 1885, he served as Grover Cleveland's Secretary of the Interior and in 1888 he was appointed as an Associate Justice of the Supreme Court. After his death in 1893, he was interred in Macon, Georgia, but true to form, he was soon reinterred in St. Peter's Cemetery in Oxford, Mississippi.

**Photograph** courtesy Kean Collection

# HELEN CARLOSS

ATTORNEY

The very first woman to argue before all of the U.S. Courts of Appeal was born in Yazoo City. Dreaming of a better life, Helen Carloss moved to Washington, D.C. in 1918 and attended law school at George Washington University, graduating in 1923. By 1928, she joined the Department of Justice, and earned a reputation as a tough attorney. Moving up quickly in the legal world, Carloss paved the way for more female lawyers to follow.

**Photograph** courtesy Mississippi University for Women

# THALIA MARA

DANCER

**"...a monumental pioneer in the history of twentieth century American dance."**

*Richard Philp, Editor in Chief Emeritus of Dance Magazine*

Thalia Mara's career as a dancer, teacher and advocate has spanned decades and countries. Trained as a young dancer by some of the Russian greats in the U.S. and Paris, she danced professionally with various companies around the world. She returned to New York to establish a solo career, performing at Radio City Music Hall, the Capitol Theater and in several Broadway shows. In 1975, she was invited to develop a professional ballet company and school in Jackson, Mississippi. In 1979 she brought the International Ballet Competition to Jackson (which has now been made the official USA home of the competition). In 1994, the Jackson Municipal Auditorium was renamed Thalia Mara Hall, and in 1998 she received the first Mayor's Arts Achievement Award, along with Eudora Welty.

Mississippi Governor Ronnie Musgrove said, "Thalia gave the gift of life, light and love to everyone and everything she touched. Thalia's life was one of celebration, and we should all be grateful that she happened our way."

**Photograph** courtesy International Ballet Competition

# JOE MEADOWS
## LONG-TERM CARE ADMINISTRATOR

We generally hear sad stories about long-term care facilities. But Gulfport native Joe Meadows is changing that. Meadows, a talented artist in his own right, purchased $400 worth of art supplies and opened a small art studio for residents at Chandler Health and Rehabilitation Center, the Alabama facility he operates. "The first night," Meadows said, "it was a packed house."

Residents of the facility now proudly display their art in the hallways. They give the works as gifts to their children and grandchildren. Meadows has shipped canvasses to as many as eight different states.

He's even getting the attention of geriatric researchers. A neurologist from The University of Alabama recently visited the facility when he heard the art therapy was improving the demeanor of combative residents.

"They feel a sense of accomplishment," Meadows said, "and the prolific painters have 'galleries' of their work in their rooms and out in the hallways."

**Photograph** by Laura Brookhart

# ROBERT ST. JOHN
AUTHOR, CHEF, RESTAURATEUR

**"St. John explores the roots of Southern hospitality with witty essays and quietly sophisticated recipes."**
Time *magazine*

Robert St. John, a native of Hattiesburg, is a 30-year veteran of the restaurant industry. For the last 23 years he has served as executive chef, president, and CEO of the Purple Parrot Café, the Crescent City Grill, Tabella, and the Mahogany Bar in Hattiesburg. St. John is a restaurateur, chef, food writer, author, and one of the nation's only food/humor columnists. He has authored eight books in the last eight years.

St. John has appeared on The Food Network, *The Travel Channel*, *National Public Radio*, *Martha Stewart Living*, and the *Turner South* network, and has been the featured chef multiple times on chefs.com and cookstr.com.

In 2009, St. John founded Extra Table, a statewide non-profit organization that helps restaurants and other businesses easily donate food to charitable organizations and mission pantries.

# REGGIE COLLIER

TRAILBLAZER

Reggie Collier, a Biloxi native, was decades ahead of his time. A quarterback who could run as well as a tailback and still throw as well as any quarterback, Collier was a prototype for the modern-day Michael Vicks.

Collier played collegiate football at the University of Southern Mississippi. In 1981, he became the first quarterback in NCAA Division I history to pass and rush for over 1,000 yards in the same season. He was in the top ten in Heisman Trophy voting that year.

In 2000, he was selected, along with Brett Favre, to the Southern Miss Team of the Century. His collegiate No. 10 jersey was retired by Southern Miss in 2008. He is currently the Coordinator of Athletic Development and Community Relations in the Southern Miss Athletics Department.

**Photograph** by Chuck Cook

BUSINESS & ENTREPRENEURS

# FRED SMITH

## FOUNDER, FEDERAL EXPRESS

FedEx Founder and Marks, Mississippi native Fred Smith comes from a long line of travelers. His grandfather, a steamboat captain, and his father, a founder of the Greyhound Bus system, left nothing but sky unclaimed. So Smith learned to fly and worked weekends as a charter pilot while studying at Yale. He was frequently asked to ferry materials for companies and wrote a class paper about the need for an express delivery service. His professor, unimpressed, marked the project with a "C" but Smith was not deterred.

After serving two tours in Vietnam, he returned home to launch his express delivery service from Memphis in 1973. With financial obstacles and the monopoly of the U.S. mail system, FedEx wasn't an overnight success, but Smith's strong work ethic and instinctual ingenuity led to one of the most brilliantly-operated companies in the world. Today, FedEx averages more than five million shipments a day across the world.

**Photograph:** FedEx founder Fred Smith in Paris announces the first order for the cargo version of Airbus' A380. Photo by Stephane de Sakutin/AFP

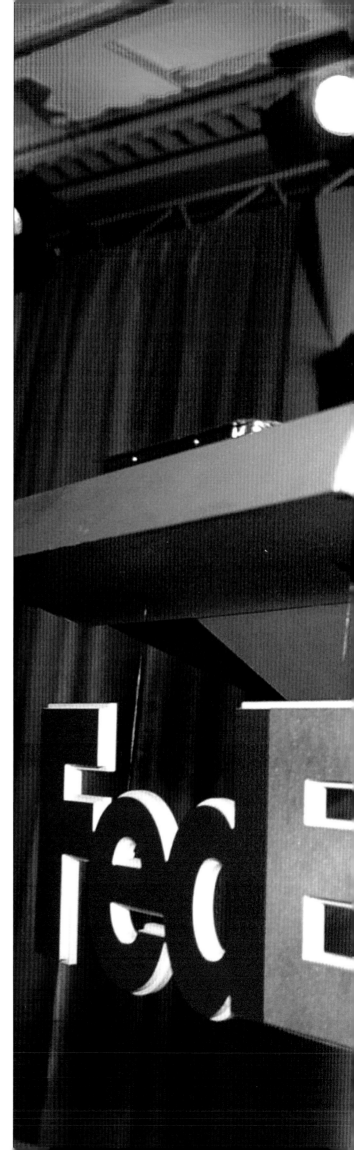

# BOB PITTMAN

FOUNDER, MTV

The Father of MTV, Bob Pittman influenced an entire generation and spawned the music video industry. At the age

of 15, he worked as a radio disc jockey in Jackson to earn money for flying lessons. From there, he became a legend, serv-

ing as program director for radio stations in Detroit, Pennsylvania, Chicago, and New York, where he brought each one

to the top. When he was asked to launch a radio station for television, he suggested they make music "visual"and gave

birth to the concept of music videos. As with other projects, the "boy wonder" enabled MTV to become the first basic

cable network to turn a profit. As CEO of MTV Networks, he also created Nick at Nite and VH-1, redesigned Nick-

elodeon, and expanded MTV into global markets. He has continued to find tremendous success with numerous business

ventures and now has more than 5,000 flight hours. Looks like that disc jockey job paid off.

**Photograph** by Marion Curtis, *Time & Life* Pictures

# JIM BARKSDALE

## ENTREPRENEUR & PHILANTHROPIST

**"If there's a penny left in my account when I die,
it will be because I miscalculated."**
*Jim Barksdale*

The son of a Jackson banker, Jim Barksdale was one of six boys in the house and competition was a mainstay. Each Sunday, his parents selected a "Boy of the Week" and honored the son with the best behavior by placing a silver dollar under his supper plate. The Barksdales taught Jim the importance of work ethic, honesty, and loyalty; those qualities led him to be one of Mississippi's wealthiest businessmen as he excelled with FedEx, McCaw Cellular Communications, and Netscape Communications Corporation. Unlike most successful businessmen, Barksdale's bank account is not how he measures success. Instead, he wants to make a difference in people's lives. He, along with his late wife, Sally, donated $5.4 million to create an Honors College at their alma mater, Ole Miss. They also donated $100 million to create a reading institute on campus in hopes of increasing literacy rates across their home state. Ole Miss Chancellor Robert Khayat noted, "Most of Jim's gifts are made anonymously, and therefore, no accurate measure of his financial contributions can be made."

**Photograph** by Alain Buu/Gamma-Rapho

# HARTLEY PEAVEY

FOUNDER & CEO, PEAVEY ELECTRONICS

No single person has had a greater impact on music and audio in the last 50 years than Hartley Peavey.

Gifted with a technical mind and a spirit for innovation, Hartley Peavey's tenacity, ingenuity and self-determination are the roots of his success. Since building his first guitar amplifier in 1957, the founder and CEO of Peavey Electronics Corporation has established a legacy of innovations, including more than 180 patents, that have helped shape the way we hear and play music.

Growing up in his father's Meridian music store, Hartley had a front-row seat for the first wave of rock & roll. But as much as he wanted to play music, he soon learned that his gifts lay not in making music, but in creating musical equipment. Today, it is virtually impossible to attend a concert, travel on an airplane, listen to a CD, or even shop at a supermarket without hearing audio that Peavey has touched along the way.

Hartley Peavey is a catalyst, a music and audio visionary who initiates change while remaining unchanged himself. Under his leadership, Peavey Electronics has ushered in great advancements in the science of sound—such as pioneering the use of computers to make better guitars, and by creating the first computer-configurable audio system, a move that triggered a digital revolution in the audio industry that his company still leads today— all while delivering the strongest quality and value proposition the industry has ever seen.

Through his creations, Hartley has enabled millions of people to enhance their lives with music, launch careers and inspire the world. His accomplishments are celebrated around the world, from patent and trademark offices to Hollywood's Rock Walk of Fame, and from the corridors of governments to the roaring applause at arenas and stadiums in more than 130 countries.

# THE CREEKMORES

TELECOMMUNICATIONS

In 1947, Wade H. Creekmore, Sr. and his cousin, Edward, acquired a small telephone company in Calhoun County. Wade, Sr.'s sons — Jimmy and Wade, Jr. — joined the family business after graduation from Ole Miss.

In 1959, the family launched Delta Telephone Company and in 1960 the Franklin Telephone Company. Jimmy managed the Louise-based Delta Telephone Company; Wade, Jr. ran the Meadville-based Franklin Telephone Company. For the next quarter century the Creekmores managed these rural telephone exchanges in several Mississippi counties — a fact that would ultimately prove crucial to the future of the company.

In 1988, the Creekmores stepped into the yet-to-be-proven mobile telephone market. They formed Cellular South and the company started with a small retail office in Gulfport, Mississippi.

In fewer than five years after the FCC began awarding licenses in the wireless industry, Cellular South had acquired several and was positioned to implement the new wireless technology.

Over the last quarter century, Cellular South, a pioneer in the wireless industry, has expanded in tandem with the astonishing growth of the wireless industry. The company has led the industry with innovative voice and data services. And the Creekmores continue their commitment to provide the same advanced services in rural areas that are available in metropolitan areas.

Community service is a top priority and a core value for Cellular South. The company established the Cellular South Foundation, an organization that has donated more than $2 million to Mississippi's eight public universities for scholarships and endowments. Cellular South also sponsors awards for the top Mississippi collegiate athlete in football, basketball and baseball.

Since 1999, Cellular South has invested more than $700 million in network infrastructure. The company is the largest privately held wireless provider in the United States. Not bad for a family business that started with a rural phone exchange in Calhoun County.

**Photograph** Mr. and Mrs. Wade H. Creekmore, Sr. (seated); (standing) Wade H. Creekmore, Jr. (left) and James "Jimmy" H. Creekmore, Sr. (right)

# GERARD GIBERT & NORMAN KATOOL

Few high tech companies have been as resilient and nimble as Ridgeland-based Venture Technologies. Led by the team of Gerard Gibert (right) and Norman Katool (left), Venture Technologies started in 1986 as a small IT solutions provider. Now, 25 years later, the company has evolved into the region's leading IT solutions consultant and cloud computing expert.

Gibert and Katool met while working together at a CPA firm. Katool was a top-flight auditor; Gibert launched the firm's IT consulting practice.

Gibert, reflecting on the early days, said, "Norman and I had an entrepreneurial itch . . . but we didn't have any money."

"We spent 16 months presenting our ideas and business plan to financial institutions and investors," Gibert said, "but banks weren't loaning money on the heels of the S&L crisis."

Undeterred, the two scraped together loans from friends and family, and obtained an SBA-backed loan that was secured by real estate owned by Gibert's in-laws.

"That land was their life's savings," he said.

The company was launched in 1986 with three employees. Now, Venture Technologies employs almost 100 with offices in Ridgeland, Memphis, Birmingham and Baton Rouge. The company owns and operates an SAS 70 Type II Certified Data Center and operates the region's only Mobile Cloud (a mobile demonstration model for cutting-edge cloud computing).

Gibert and Katool credit their success to Venture Technologies' employees. "I attribute our success to our talented, loyal staff," Katool said. "We've been blessed to retain the industry's best talent."

But the real secret to the company's success has been its ability to adjust to an ever-changing technology landscape. As Gibert noted, "The only constant in our industry is change."

Under the leadership of Gibert & Katool, Venture Technologies is sure to remain on top.

**Photo** by Jimmy Winstead

# SAM STEIN

IMMIGRANT, PEDDLER, RETAILER

Sam Stein, a Russian immigrant, arrived in New York in 1905 with $43 in his pocket. He dreamed of a better life. After traveling down the Mississippi River, Sam Stein chose to settle in Greenville, Mississippi, where he began making his rounds to sharecroppers' cabins. With a thick Russian accent, Stein carried a sack of inexpensive household goods to peddle. Eventually, he purchased a horse and buggy. And in 1908, he opened his first store. As the business grew, Stein began specializing in clothes, shoes, fabric, and household items. His store was always geared toward, and priced for, the working-class customer. Sam Stein continued to operate his store until his sudden death in 1933.

From this humble beginning, Stein Mart — a national retail chain with more than 260 stores — was born.

**Photograph** courtesy Stein Mart

# JAY STEIN

CHAIRMAN, STEIN MART

Jay Stein, grandson of Sam Stein (see facing page), grew up in the family store. He often worked there as a teen, after school and on weekends. In 1967, after returning from NYU, Jay began working full-time in the family's Greenville store. He and his father, Jake, often struggled with their very different managing styles. Jake worked by instinct and without paperwork, while Jay wanted to work with structure, planning and formal guidelines. After ten years of conflicting styles, they decided to open a second store in Memphis. This store was considered a test for Jay. He would pass or fail on his own. Jay passed with flying colors. The Memphis store was a success, and Jay began opening more store locations in the South and across America.

Jay Stein became President and CEO of Stein Mart, Inc., just a year after the Memphis store's opening. Under his leadership, Stein Mart has become a billion dollar franchise with some 265 stores in about 30 states.

**Photograph** courtesy Stein Mart

# BILL RAYBURN

CO-FOUNDER, FNC, INC.

The University of Mississippi has given birth to many dreams, including that of FNC co-founder William Rayburn. During a lunch meeting in the mid-1990s, when residential mortgage lenders were struggling with archaic systems to assess the true value of a property, Rayburn asked a group of colleagues (and future partners), "What if we could automate the way appraisals are processed? What if we could convert paper to data to knowledge that mortgage lenders could use to make better loans faster? That would be fantastic!"

Along with Robert Dorsey, John Johnson and Dennis Tosh, a dream team was formed. Today, the nation's largest residential mortgage lenders and servicers depend on FNC's Collateral Management System® for compliance and efficiency; and the company has been recognized as one of the most rapidly growing tech companies in America.

In 2011, Rayburn was inducted into the Mississippi Technology Alliance's Innovators Hall of Fame.

Rayburn and his co-founders remain firmly committed to Mississippi, lending support to countless philanthropic projects across the state as they broaden their economic footprint.

All thanks to a paper napkin and an Ole Miss professor who dared to ask, "What if?"

**Photograph** courtesty FNC, Inc.

# FRED CARL, JR.
## PRESIDENT & CEO, VIKING

When Fred Carl's wife asked him to find a better stove for her kitchen, he realized there were very few options for top-of-the-line residential appliances. As a fourth-generation contractor, he saw a niche to fill. It took years to convince the rest of the world that they needed high-end, commercial-grade appliances tweaked for home kitchens, but he followed his dream and created the Mercedes of stoves. Now, his Viking Range Corporation delivers kitchen appliances around the globe. The brand has expanded into all aspects of the fine dining, culinary experience. Despite tremendous commercial success, Carl has remained loyal to his hometown of Greenwood. There, he maintains the Viking Corporate offices, which occupy more than 600,000 square feet for Viking production and distribution.

**Photograph** courtesy Viking

# AUBREY PATTERSON

BANKER & CIVIC LEADER

When Aubrey Patterson started work for the Bank of Mississippi in 1972 as an assistant vice president, no one could have guessed he would lead a relatively small northeast Mississippi community bank through a series of mergers, acquisitions and growth that would place the bank, known today as BancorpSouth, in the top 75 commercial banks chartered in the United States.. Under Patterson's leadership — and vision — BancorpSouth has grown into a full-service financial services company with over $13 billion in assets, more than 4,000 employees and approximately 300 locations in nine states.

Having once been described by an industry journalist as possessing, "a quiet demeanor, but with an analytical mind, a competitive spirit and clearly formed ideas about banking," Patterson views his career as a calling and his life's chosen work. Mr. Patterson also serves on the Financial Services Roundtable Board of Directors (the Roundtable represents 100 of the largest integrated financial services companies providing banking, insurance, and investment products and services to the American consumer).

Robert Khayat said, "Concurrently, with Aubrey's leadership of the bank, he has emerged as a leader in Tupelo — and across the state and the nation." Patterson, who has held innumerable civic and industry positions, served as chairman of the American Bankers Association in 2002. Passionate about efforts to improve education, he was appointed by Governor Haley Barbour in 2004 to an eleven-year term on the Mississippi Board of Trustees of Institutions of Higher Learning, the governing board for Mississippi's eight state universities.

# VICTOR H. "HU" MEENA, JR.

PRESIDENT & CEO, CELLULAR SOUTH

In 1987 Hu Meena opened Cellular South's first office on the Mississippi Gulf Coast. The company launched cellular service in February of 1988. In 1990, Meena was promoted to vice president of operations and development for Cellular South. And in 1997, he was named president of Cellular South, Inc., a wholly owned subsidiary of Telapex, Inc.

Since those early days with a dozen employees on the Coast, Cellular South has grown to become the largest privately held wireless carrier (and the ninth largest overall) in the nation with over 1,000 employees.

Under Meena's leadership, Cellular South has garnered dozens of national and regional awards for safety, leadership and innovation. And you can bet that Meena has big plans for the company's future.

Meena serves as chairman of the board of the Associated Carrier Group, a wireless device purchasing cooperative made up of more than 35 rural wireless carriers, and Chairman of the Board of Rural Cellular Association (RCA). He is married to Ashley Creekmore Meena and they have three sons, Victor Matthew, Wade Albert and Lee Creekmore.

**Photograph** courtesy Cellular South

# MICHAEL W. HARLAN

CO-FOUNDER, U.S. CONCRETE, INC.

I n August 1998, Oxford native Michael Harlan partnered with Main Street Equity Ventures, a Houston-based venture capital firm, to found U.S. Concrete, Inc. Harlan served as Chief Financial Officer from 1999 until 2003 when he assumed the role of Chief Operating Officer. In 2006, he was elected to the Board of Directors and in 2007, he was named President and Chief Executive Officer. Under his leadership, U.S. Concrete grew to be one of the largest concrete producers in the U.S. with almost $1 billion in annual revenue and over 3,000 employees. After graduating magna cum laude from the University of Mississippi in 1982, Harlan began his career with an international public accounting firm. Prior to founding U.S. Concrete, he participated in the creation of two other publicly-traded companies, one of which is now the third largest solid waste management company in the U.S.

Harlan serves on the Board of Directors of the National Ready Mixed Concrete Association and is the Chairman of the Board of Trustees for the RMC Research and Education Foundation. He is also a member of the National Steering Committee of the Concrete Industry Management Education Program where he serves as an officer and a member of the Executive Committee. In 2009, he became a member of the Advisory Board for the University of Houston Honors College.

In addition, Harlan was a founding Director of Waste Connections, Inc., a publicly-traded solid waste management company, and he currently serves as the Lead Independent Director and Chairman of the Audit Committee.

310

# DANIEL O. CONWILL, IV

INVESTMENT BANKER

Daniel O. Conwill IV is a founder, Chairman of the Board and CEO of Global Hunter Securities, LLC. He also runs the investment banking group at the company. Prior to forming GHS, Mr. Conwill was Executive Vice President and Co-Director of Corporate Finance at Jefferies & Company, Inc. While at Jefferies & Co, Conwill founded its oil and gas investment banking group in 1993 and managed that group until his departure in 2005. During that time, the group raised over $15 billion in over 100 private and public equity and debt transactions and completed over 70 merger and acquisition transactions totaling over $10 billion in transaction value. Prior to joining Jefferies in 1993, Conwill was a Managing Director in corporate finance at Howard, Weil, Labouisse, Friedrichs, Inc. Conwill's professional career started in the tax department with Arthur Andersen & Co.

Conwill, a Gulfport native, received his Bachelors and Masters Degrees in Accounting from the University of Mississippi and has a law degree from the University of Mississippi School of Law.

**Photograph** by Kate S. Elkins

# GAIL PITTMAN

ARTISTS, ENTREPRENEUR

**"Color makes me smile, it inspires me, and for this reason I paint designs that make my heart sing!"**

*Gail Pittman*

Though she would not have an artistic career for many years, Gail Pittman's first works of art were created when she was in preschool: she colored her entire bedroom in crayons and used shaving cream (taken from her father) to create clouds. Years later, she graduated from Ole Miss with a degree in elementary education, and taught school in Jackson for five years before deciding to stay home with her children. It was at this stage in her life that she rediscovered her creativity, hand-painting her own dinnerware. It wasn't long before she started her own company, and moved away from the kitchen table to form a nationally recognized business. Pittman has designed for celebrities such as Katie Couric, Paula Dean, and fellow Mississippians Oprah Winfrey and Faith Hill. Many of her designs can be found in casinos and restaurants across the country, and she served as the Creative Director for Southern Living at Home from 2005 to 2010.

**Photograph** courtesy Gail Pittman

# STEPHEN JOHNSTON

ENTREPRENEUR

**"Stephen Johnston is extremely energetic and biased toward action. He is a leader."**

*John Palmer*

Stephen Johnston joined Mississippi company SmartSynch in 2000. Since then, as CEO, he's led the company's efforts to raise over $90 million in venture capital — the largest amount ever by a single entity in the state.

SmartSynch's technology enables utility companies (and consumers) to monitor energy usage in real time. The company's products and services help utility providers spot and stop "leaks," increasing efficiency and normalizing energy loads during peak use.

What's it all mean? SmartSynch is at the center of what will be this century's largest investment — a six trillion dollar expenditure in energy infrastructure.

Currently, huge amounts of energy sent over electric power lines are wasted. SmartSynch's technology will help reduce that waste. Environmentally sound, yes. Fiscally sound, too. According to some estimates, the United States could save over $75 billion per year through enhanced smart grid technology.

Under Johnston's leadership, the company could change the way energy use is monitored and regulated. And SmartSynch might just be Mississippi's next publicly traded company.

**Photograph** courtesy The University of Mississippi

# CAMPBELL MCCOOL

ENTREPRENEUR

In 1992 Campbell McCool formed McCool Communications in Atlanta with no clients and $20,000 in seed capital. Over the course of ten years McCool Communications grew into one of the Southeast's most respected boutique advertising and public relations firms. Clients included CNN, Bridgestone, TNT Latin America, E-Z-GO Textron, Mizuno, SmartSynch, The PGA of America, Agentware, Turner Home Satellite, ExpoExchange, Worldspan and many others.

During the late 1990s McCool Communications won countless Addys, Effies, and other industry awards, as well as signing on dozens of new clients. "If we got invited to a pitch, we stood a good chance of winning," McCool recalled. After turning down several buyout offers, the company was acquired in 2001 by publicly held Maxxcomm, a Canadian holding company that owned agencies across North America.

McCool moved back to Mississippi in 2003 to help launch Blueprint Mississippi. He continues to use his marketing expertise with various entrepreneurial ventures, including The Barksdale Reading Institute and The Gertrude C. Ford Center at Ole Miss. McCool served as the initial co-founder of The Rowan Oak Society and he sits on the board of the Greater Oxford-Lafayette Community Foundation. He is now the Chief Marketing Officer for Jackson-based SmartSynch.

**Photograph** by Leighton McCool

# ED MEEK

ENTREPRENEUR & PHILANTHROPIST

The first in his family to attend college, Ed Meek directed the University of Mississippi public relations department for nearly three decades, while simultaneously building a magazine and trade show empire. Meek founded the Tupelo Furniture Market (now the largest in America). He also built a Las Vegas trade show that is the largest hospitality event of its kind in the western hemisphere — known internationally as "The Show."

Meek's lifelong friend Robert Khayat said, "Genius is found in Ed's creation of an annual trade show that attracted 50,000 people each year to Las Vegas."

In 2008, Meek sold his business to a global media company. He and his wife, Becky, donated $5.3 million to the University of Mississippi to launch the Meek School of Journalism & New Media.

**Photograph:** Ed Meek (right) with Will Norton, Jr. (left), Dean of The Meek School of Journalism and New Media.
Photo courtesy of The University of Mississippi

# JOE ESTESS

ENTREPRENEUR, CEO

Diversify.

That term is thrown around a lot in business circles. With five companies under his belt, Joe Estess brings new meaning to the word. The Magnolia Business Centre is the corporate headquarters for the five Tupelo-based companies founded by Estess: Vector Transport, Eagle Capital, Heritage Memorial Funding, Timberlake Foods and Southern Belle Refrigerated. Estess recognized customer needs, filled those niche markets, and created jobs in north Mississippi when they were needed most. The conglomerate is ranked among the top private companies in the state by the *Mississippi Business Journal*. Estess and his host of companies have had an enormous economic impact on the region. All five companies continue to be managed by family members.

Recently, Estess recorded a series of podcasts called "The Success Factor with Joe Estess," which provide listeners with easy tips for building and managing a business.

# TOXEY HAAS

## CEO OF MOSSY OAK

**"My mind belongs to my work, my heart belongs to my family, but my soul belongs to the woods."**
*Toxey Haas*

It all began in West Point, Mississippi, with a fistful of dirt. Obsessed with the notion of getting closer to animals, Toxey Haas gathered up a bag of leaves, sticks, and dirt from under his favorite hunting tree, walked into a fabric factory, dropped it on the counter, and asked, "Can you print fabric that looks like this stuff?" He was onto something big.

Haas realized the best camouflage would use natural elements—dirt, leaves, bark, and limbs. Consequently, Mossy Oak's patterns have evolved to become almost lifelike. Haas revolutionized the way people thought about camouflage, and his company was the first to use computer technology to produce their patterns. In 2009, Haas was honored by Ducks Unlimited as a Hero of Conservation, for his efforts in getting people outdoors, planting and preserving. As founder and CEO of Mossy Oak, Haas has overseen the development of some of the most popular and effective camouflage patterns in the country, allowing outdoor enthusiasts to hide in plain sight.

# MIKE STEWART

DOG BREEDER, TRAINER

**"Mike Stewart breeds $12,000 dogs that can hunt and play."**

Forbes

One of Mike Stewart's clients flies into Oxford on a private jet from Alaska. Another is the CEO of an international gold and copper mining company. They all gather regularly at Wildrose Kennels — 143 acres outside Oxford, Mississippi — where some of the world's best canine companions are bred and trained.

Stewart has trained dogs for over 30 years. The former chief of police at the University of Mississippi, he quips, "College kids are just like dogs. They learn best from repetition and consistency." Stewart has a backlog of orders for pups that numbers in the hundreds. Prices for Wildrose dogs (they deal only in English sporting Labradors) range from $1,500 for puppies to $15,000 for a finished dog (those that have trained at Wildrose and have hunted 1000-plus fallen birds). Stewart was featured on the cover of *Forbes* magazine in April of 2009.

**Photograph** by Scott Rob, Commonwealth Productions

JOURNALISTS

# SHEPARD SMITH

FOX NEWS ANCHOR

Holly Springs native Shepard Smith was a typical Mississippi boy. The son of a school teacher and a cotton merchant, Smith attended both Marshall Academy and Ole Miss. After working his way up in the news world, he joined the start-up Fox News Network in 1996. He is one of America's top television news anchors, regularly voted one of the most trustworthy announcers. He currently hosts the "Fox Report with Shepard Smith" and "Studio B" on the Fox News Network, where he regularly expresses strong opinions when covering stories like Hurricane Katrina and waterboarding. He never misses a chance to plug his alma mater, Ole Miss.

**Photograph** courtesy University of Mississippi

# ROBIN ROBERTS
GOOD MORNING AMERICA

Robin Roberts, born and raised in Pass Christian, Mississippi, is one of the most successful television broadcasters in America today. She serves as the co-anchor of ABC's "Good Morning America." After college, Roberts moved to Hattiesburg, Mississippi, and began her broadcasting career. She served as reporter and sports anchor for WDAM-TV. She went on to become a sportscaster for ESPN, where she coined her catchphrase, "Go on with your bad self!" Roberts has won three Emmy Awards for her work in broadcasting and drove the pace car for the 2010 Indianapolis 500.

**Photograph:** Mississippi native Robin Roberts at Kensington Palace and Gardens in England, during the 2011 Royal Wedding. Photo by Donna Svennevik/ABC

# HAZEL BRANNON SMITH

NEWSPAPER EDITOR & PUBLISHER

**"Laws were made to protect the weak in our society from the strong."**
*Hazel Brannon Smith*

When Hazel Brannon Smith graduated from the University of Alabama with a B.A. in Journalism and bought the local newspaper in Durant, Mississippi, she could never have known that she would later own four newspapers in Mississippi and be the recipient of a Pulitzer Prize. She was, in fact, the first woman to ever win a Pulitzer Prize for editorial writing. Her published opposition to the White Citizens' Council earned her the Pulitzer in 1964. She later received other awards for her biting editorials against social injustice in Mississippi, including awards from the National Federation of Press Women and the Herrick Award for Editorial Writing.

**Photograph** © Bettmann/CORBIS

# LARRY SPEAKES
PRESIDENTIAL PRESS SECRETARY

*T*he *Oxford Eagle* gave Larry Speakes his start. That's where he served as editor after graduating from Ole Miss. He was there for one year before taking over as managing editor for his hometown paper in Cleveland, and later as general manager and editor for the *Leland Progress*.

In 1968, Speakes headed to Washington as press secretary to Mississippi Senator James Eastland. Once in DC, he earned the respect of America's highest officials. He has worked directly for Presidents Nixon, Ford, and Reagan, the latter for whom he served as assistant to the president and principal press secretary.

**Photograph** White House Press Secretary Larry Speaks speaking in White House press room about arms shipments to Iran.
Photo by Dirck Halstead/*Time & Life* Pictures

# HODDING CARTER, JR.

DELTA DEMOCRAT TIMES

Hodding Carter, Jr. was once fired from the Associated Press and told he would never make it as a journalist. That was before he published more than 20 books, built a lifelong and substantial newspaper career in the Mississippi Delta, and won a Pulitzer Prize for Editorial Writing. An early champion of civil rights, most of Carter's writings focused on race in the South, examining with precision the causes and effects of racial segregation. In the end, he became known as a hero and a legend to all people, both black and white. Carter said, "If I have gained anything in life, it is a belief in the soul and the destiny of man."

**Photograph** by Robert W. Kelley, *Time & Life* Pictures

# CRAIG CLAIBORNE

GOURMET, NEW YORK TIMES

**"I don't take this cuisine business all that seriously. Food is a matter of pleasure."**

*Craig Claiborne*

Craig Claiborne is to food what Martha Stewart is to home entertaining. A southern boy with a passion for cooking, Claiborne left the South to explore the wonders of the world — and that meant food. He served as editor of *Gourmet* magazine. Then he landed a job as the *New York Times'* first food editor. He also published more than 20 cookbooks and gave birth to an era when men could wear aprons and share recipes as freely as women. It took half a lifetime to reconcile with his Mississippi roots, but when he did, a little bit of magic happened. Published near the end of his career, *Craig Claiborne's Southern Cooking* celebrates the culinary talents of trained chefs and southern house-wives alike and brings Mississippi recipes to the center of America's table.

**Photograph** Gourmet and author Craig Claiborne in his kitchen espousing low-salt diet.. Photo by Arthur Schatz/*Time & Life* Pictures

# DAN GOODGAME

TIME, FORTUNE SMALL BUSINESS

At Ole Miss, Pascagoula native Dan Goodgame majored in journalism and edited *The Daily Mississippian*. He then attended Oxford University as a Rhodes Scholar. Known as a talented raconteur who enjoys coaxing stories out of people who are not big talkers, Goodgame has worked as a foreign correspondent, White House correspondent, Washington Bureau chief, and top editor for *Time* magazine.

He served as editor of *Fortune Small Business*, a trade magazine with over one million subscribers. Under his leadership, the publication won national awards for excellence.

Goodgame is also the co-author of *Marching in Place* — a book about President George H.W. Bush.

# CHARLES OVERBY

THE FREEDOM FORUM & NEWSEUM

**"I believe my life's mission is to encourage people. There isn't enough of that going on in the world."**

*Charles Overby*

As a boy, Jackson native Charles Overby shared a paper route with his brother. They pooled their money with their mother's meager paychecks to make ends meet. But when Overby won a statewide contest to sell the most papers, he earned a life-altering trip to Europe and realized he could do anything he set his mind to.

He worked his way through Ole Miss, where he excelled in journalism. After graduation, he worked for Senator John Stennis and became a Washington correspondent for southern newspapers. After he was named editor of *The Clarion-Ledger* in Jackson, Overby led a major news and editorial campaign on the need for significant education reform in Mississippi. The paper won the Pulitzer Prize for Public Service.

Today, Overby is one of the most well-respected communications professionals in America. He serves as chairman and CEO of The Freedom Forum and CEO of the Newseum in Washington, DC.

In 2007, The Overby Center for Southern Journalism and Politics opened on the Ole Miss campus. The Center's mission is to create better understanding of politics and the media and the role of the First Amendment in our democracy.

**Photograph** Charles Overby stands in the upper level of the Newsum that features an actual news chopper.
Photo by Michael Williamson/*The Washington Post*

# SAMIR HUSNI

MR. MAGAZINE

**"The country's leading magazine expert."**
*Forbes ASAP*

The man who loves magazines, Samir Afif Husni, aka, Mr. Magazine™, is the founder and director of the Magazine Innovation Center at the University of Mississippi. He is also a professor of journalism, an author and collector of new magazine launches in the United States.

The Associated Press wrote of Husni, "He has enough *Time* on his hands to be a real *Details* man. He's got *Allure*, and he is completely in *Vogue* – a real *Cosmopolitan* kind of guy. His *People* skills are formidable. He has a good sense of *Self*, has a *Spin* for everything and knows all about *Us* . . . . Husni is a maestro of magazines, a potentate of periodicals who has parlayed his interest into a career of academics, consulting and just plain reading."

When Husni is not in his office, he is at the newsstands, continuing his childhood hobby of finding and buying first editions of new magazines. His collection today is over 26,000 copies of premier issues of magazines. It's no wonder *Adweek* referred to Husni as The Prince of the Premiere.

**Photograph** courtesy The University of Mississippi

# CURTIS WILKIE

JOURNALIST, AUTHOR

**"One of the nation's most distinguished journalists."**
*David Halberstam*

As a newspaper reporter and editor, Curtis Wilkie covered Mississippi's Freedom Summer of 1964, Martin Luther King's last campaign, Robert Kennedy's Delta tour, the 1976 Jimmy Carter election, and the Byron de la Beckwith conviction. During a 26-year stint with the *Boston Globe*, Wilkie served as a correspondent from Washington, Jerusalem, and New Orleans. Roy Blount, Jr. said "Curtis Wilkie has been the right man in the right place at an uncanny number of extraordinary times."

Wilkie is author of *Arkansas Mischief, Dixie: A Personal Odyssey Through Events that Shaped the Modern South*, and *The Fall of the House of Zeus*. Of Wilkie's *The Fall of the House of Zeus*, John Evans — proprietor of Lemuria Books — said, "No one since Willie Morris has written so poignantly about the South."

*Zeus* broke sales records in 2010 among Mississippi independent bookstores.

**Photograph** courtesy The University of Mississippi

# JOHN T. EDGE

JOURNALIST, AUTHOR

**"To call John T. Edge a food writer is like saying Herman Melville wrote booklets on fishing."**

*Jack Pendarvis*

Everyone knows you can't separate southern culture from southern cooking. Down here, it's all about the food. And that's what John T. Edge celebrates. Edge, an Oxford resident, writes a monthly column, "United Tastes," for the *New York Times*. He is a contributing editor at *Garden & Gun*. He is a longtime columnist for the *Oxford American*. And he was a contributing editor at *Gourmet*.

With his extraordinary talent for analyzing the connection between food and folklore, Edge's work has garnered international attention. He has served as culinary curator for the weekend edition of NPR's *All Things Considered*, and he has been featured on dozens of television shows from *CBS Sunday Morning* to *Iron Chef*.

Keep an eye on Edge. Despite five James Beard Foundation Award nominations, despite six published books, despite seven works appearing in the *Best Food Writing*, most think John T. Edge is just getting started.

**Photograph** by Angie Mosier

# TURNER CATLEDGE

NEW YORK TIMES

Turner Catledge's first job was reporting for *The Neshoba Democrat*. In 1922, he was appointed editor of the *Tunica Times* where he wrote many an unpopular column, including a series of anti-KKK articles. He was hired away by the *New York Times*. Catledge, a New Prospect native, worked for the venerable newspaper for more than 40 years. Catledge was appointed managing editor of the *Times* in 1951, followed by an executive editor appointment in 1964. Under his direction, the newspaper won dozens of Pulitzer Prizes. In 1968, he was appointed vice president of the *New York Times* corporation. Catledge's papers are preserved in the Mitchell Memorial Library at Mississippi State University.

# WILLIAM RASPBERRY

THE WASHINGTON POST

William Raspberry, a popular syndicated columnist for *The Washington Post*, said "We had two of everything in Okolona, Mississippi. One for whites and one for blacks." He was describing his hometown, Okolona, during his childhood in the 1930s and 1940s. Race was such a critical component of his southern culture, Raspberry spent his entire career writing honest, controversial opinions about it. That practice earned him a Pulitzer Prize for Commentary in 1994 and encouraged countless readers to change the way they think.

**Photograph** by Milly Moorhead West

# BILL MINOR
JOURNALIST

Bill Minor is a legend. After he graduated from Tulane University in 1943 with a degree in journalism, he served the U.S. in World War II as a naval combat officer. Then, he joined the staff of *The Times-Picayune* in New Orleans. In 1947, he was assigned as the newspaper's Mississippi correspondent in Jackson, Mississippi. Covering the civil rights era and a wide variety of other major news stories, Minor held this position for thirty years. Since his retirement he remains in Jackson and has launched a career as a statewide political columnist, a position which he today still holds.

**Photograph** Bill Minor at the Neshoba County Courthouse. Photo by Marianne Todd/Getty Images

# JAMES AUTRY

EDITOR, POET, AUTHOR

James Autry is the author of ten books that range from business leadership to christianity. His first two books were books of poetry, *Nights Under a Tin Roof* and *Life After Mississippi*. Autry was also the CEO of Meredith Corporation's magazine group. At the time of his retirement in 1991, he was regarded as one of the most successful and respected magazine publishing executives in the U.S.

Autry began with Meredith Corporation in 1960 as copy editor of *Better Homes & Gardens* magazine, and by the time he retired was senior vice president of Meredith Corporation and president of its magazine group - a $500 million operation with over 900 employees.

**Photograph** by Judy Griesedieck/*Time & Life* Pictures

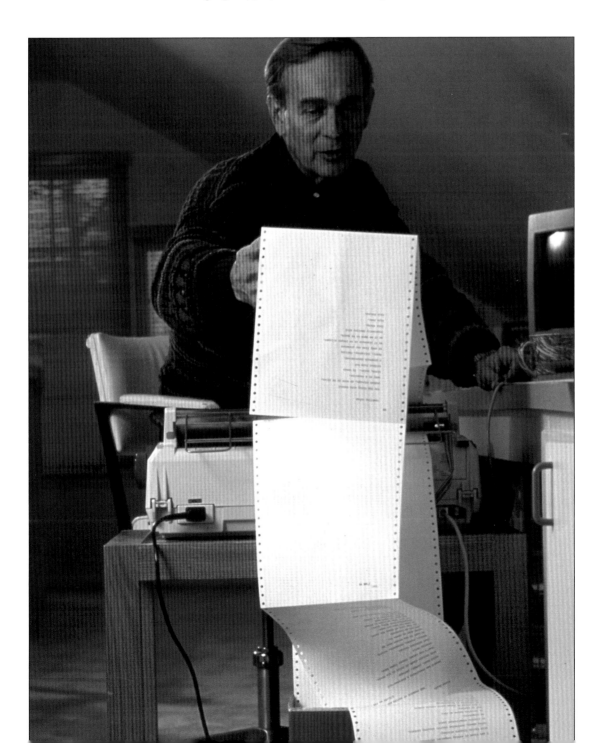

# JERRY MITCHELL

Jerry W. Mitchell is an award-winning investigative reporter. As a reporter for *The Clarion-Ledger*, he convinced authorities to reopen seemingly cold murder cases from the Civil Rights Era, prompting one colleague to call him "the South's Simon Wiesentha."

Mitchell's investigations have led to the arrest of several Klansmen and prompted authorities to reexamine numerous killings during the civil rights era. In 1996, he was portrayed in the Rob Reiner film, *Ghosts of Mississippi*, about the murder of Medgar Evers and the belated effort to bring killer Byron De La Beckwith to justice. He was featured in The Learning Channel documentary *Civil Rights Martyrs* that aired in February 2000 and was a consultant for the Discovery Channel documentary *Killed by the Klan* which aired in 1999.

In 2009, he received a genius grant from the MacArthur Foundation.

**Photograph** by James Patterson

# RICK CLEVELAND

Rick Cleveland counts two very important influences on his life and work. His father, who was also a sports writer and an inductee in the Mississippi Sports Hall of Fame, encouraged him to write. So too did his other influence, Willie Morris, with whom he shared a long friendship. Cleveland has covered sports for *The Clarion-Ledger* since 1979. He has published two books: *It's More Than a Game*, a collection of his articles from 1985 to 1999, and *Vaught: The Man and His Legacy*, about legendary coach Johnny Vaught. In 2011 Cleveland was awarded the Richard Wright Literary Excellence Award from the Natchez Literary and Cinema Celebration, presented to "a living author with strong Mississippi connections whose body of written work is exemplary."

# DOUGLAS BLACKMON

JOURNALIST, AUTHOR

**"A terrific journalist and gifted writer, Blackmon is fearless
in going wherever the research leads him."**

*Atlanta Magazine*

A small-town Delta boy. That's what Douglas Blackmon was when he penned his first newspaper article at the age of 12 for Leland's local *Progress*, years before serving as *The Wall Street Journal*'s Atlanta bureau chief. Growing up in rural Mississippi, Blackmon watched closely and tried to figure out the long and tangled history of race. For the last 20 years, Blackmon has written extensively about the American quandary of color, exploring the integration of schools during his childhood in a Mississippi Delta farm town, lost episodes of the civil rights movement, and, repeatedly, the dilemma of how a contemporary society should grapple with a troubled past.

Blackmon's nonfiction book, *Slavery by Another Name*, won the 2009 Pulitzer Prize.

**Photograph** by Michael A. Schwartz

# RHETA GRIMSLEY JOHNSON

JOURNALIST, AUTHOR

**"Rheta Grimsley Johnson writes with nothing short of beauty about childhood, lost loves, sad dogs, and everything else worth knowing about."**

*Rick Bragg on* Enchanted Evening Barbie

Acolumnist for over 30 years, Rheta Grimsley Johnson was the winner of the Ernie Pyle Award for human interest reporting, and in 1986 was inducted into the Scripps Howard Newspapers Editorial Hall of Fame. The author of *Poor Man's Provence: Finding Myself in Cajun Louisiana* and *Good Grief: The Story of Charles M. Schulz*, in 2011, Johnson released her memoir, *Enchanted Evening Barbie*.

Today, Johnson's columns are syndicated in over 50 papers nationwide.

# PEARL RIVERS

## ELIZA JANE POITEVENT HOLBROOK NICHOLSON

Eliza Jane Poitevant Holbrook Nicholson was the first woman publisher of a major newspaper in the United States. She moved with her family to Picayune in Pearl River County, from whence she took her nom de plume, Pearl Rivers. After the Civil War, she began to submit her poems, which were published in literary sheets in New Orleans and New York. In 1866 the New Orleans daily *The Picayune* began to publish her poetry. Alva Holbrook, the co-owner of the paper, asked her to become the literary editor. She took the job against her family's wishes and became the first woman journalist in Louisiana. She eventually married Holbrook, even though his ex-wife once attacked her with a gun and a bottle of rum. When Holbrook died, he left the paper to her. Although it was facing bankruptcy, Rivers took it on. With the help of business manager George Nicholson (whom she married in 1878), they turned it around and made it one of the most successful newspapers in the South. She was a pioneer in publishing, making the paper a leading journal by adding much of what are considered modern newspaper elements now: stories on women, children's pages, poetry, a gossip columnist, literary stories, chalk illustrations, and advertising boxes. She died in 1896 of influenza.

**Photograph** courtesy *The Times-Picayune*

# GEORGE MCLEAN

PUBLISHER, PHILANTHROPIST

**"We believe that a newspaper is a public trust and that it should constantly serve the people to the greatest possible extent."**

*George McLean*

Locally referred to as "The Tupelo Miracle," Tupelo's local newspaper, the *Northeast Mississippi Daily Journal* (formerly the *Tupelo Daily Journal*), is a locally owned newspaper and its profits go right back into improving the Tupelo community. How does this happen in today's cutthroat business world? George McLean. In 1935, he published the failing, bi-weekly paper, and turned into a thriving, daily publication. He used the paper's profits for his local community, creating the Tupelo's Community Development Foundation. It has been instrumental in building highways, encouraging and bolstering education, and supporting local business. McLean's legacy lives on, with the George McLean Institute for Community Development at the University of Mississippi; this organization uses the "Tupelo model" to encourage community development all over north Mississippi.

**Photograph** by Milly Moorhead West

# ELLIS NASSOUR

AUTHOR, JOURNALIST

Voted one of *Time* Magazine's Persons of the Year in 2006, Ellis Nassour is the author of several books, including *Rock Opera: the Creation of Jesus Christ, Superstar, Patsy Cline* and *Honky Tonk Angel: The Intimate Story of Patsy Cline*. Born and raised in Vicksburg, he attended Ole Miss and eventually moved to New York to pursue his dreams of writing. With several books under his belt, his *Honky Tonk Angel* was used as the basis for *Honky Tonk Angel: The Patsy Cline Musical*, which premiered in 2005 and was subsequently mounted around the world on tour.

Nassour is also an international arts media journalist, as well as associate producer of the Drama Desk Award.

In 2004, he donated the Mamie and Ellis Nassour Arts and Entertainment Collection to the J.D. Williams Library at Ole Miss.

**Photograph** by Linda Lenzi

SOCIAL REFORMERS

# JAMES MEREDITH

CIVIL RIGHTS ACTIVIST, AUTHOR

**"I think they'll take care of me."**

*James Meredith, on his fellow African-Americans*

The year, 1962. The campus, Ole Miss. James Meredith was under the protection of federal marshals when he became the first African-American student to be admitted to the university. His entrance wasn't well-received by the traditionalists who feared change more than death. Riots broke out. More than 30,000 troops tried to restore calm. Shots were fired. Two people died. And the entire world watched as Meredith kept a straight face and entered the doors of the Lyceum. He graduated from Ole Miss one year later, by combining credits from the all-black Jackson State, and he published a memoir called *Three Years in Mississippi*. Meredith remained a leader throughout the civil rights movement, even after he was shot by a sniper during his solitary protest "March Against Fear." One generation later, thanks to fearless leaders such as Meredith, his son Joe earned his Ph.D. in business from the University of Mississippi.

**Photograph** courtesy The University of Mississippi

# MEDGAR EVERS

## CIVIL RIGHTS ACTIVIST

**"You can kill a man, but you can't kill an idea."**

*Medgar Evers*

The 1963 shooting of civil rights activist Medgar Evers may have been the tipping point that resulted in the Civil Rights Act of 1964. After graduating from college, Evers organized local NAACP affiliates in Philadelphia, Mississippi. When the Supreme Court ruled in favor of desegregation, Evers applied for law school at Ole Miss. He was denied admission, but his efforts attracted national attention and led him to Jackson, where he became the first Mississippi state field secretary for the NAACP. He worked diligently trying to register black voters and investigate hate crimes, including the murder of 14-year-old Emmett Till. Evers' activism made him a target for Mississippi segregationists, and after receiving numerous threats and attacks, he was fatally shot in the back on June 12, 1963. Despite clear evidence, it took nearly 31 years for justice to prevail. In 1994, Evers' murderer, Byron de la Beckwith, was finally convicted and sentenced to life in prison, where he died in 2001 at the age of 80.

**Photograph** NAACP Field Secretary Medgar Evers in Jackson, Mississippi circa 1960.
Photo by Michael Ochs Archive

# FANNIE LOU HAMER
CIVIL RIGHTS ACTIVIST

**"If Fannie Lou Hamer had had the same opportunities that Martin Luther King had, then we would have had a female Martin Luther King."**

*Kay Mills, Hamer biographer*

Fannie Lou Hamer played a significant role in the Civil Rights Movement in the South. She helped organize Freedom Summer, she served as Vice-Chair of the Mississippi Freedom Democratic Party, and she was seated as a member of Mississippi's delegation to the Democratic National Convention in 1968. When a man came to her church in 1962 to get blacks to register to vote, she realized exactly how unfair life in the South was for her race, saying "I had never heard, until 1962, that black people could register and vote."

"I guess if I'd had any sense, I'd have been a little scared," Hamer said when signing up to vote, "but what was the point of being scared? The only thing they [white people] could do was kill me, and it seemed they'd been trying to do that a little bit at a time since I could remember."

Though she passed away from cancer in 1977, her legacy lives on. In 2009, an opera titled *Dark River* about Hamer's life and activism premiered in California.

**Photograph**: Fannie Lou Hamer (left) is joined by the parents of slain civil rights worker, Michael Schwerner in Atlantic City, New Jersey, 1964, during the protest outside of Convention Hall over seating of Mississippi delegates.
Photo by Robert Abbott Sengstack

# AARON HENRY

CIVIL RIGHTS ACTIVIST

**"I think that every time a man stands for an ideal or speaks out against injustice,
he sends out a tiny ripple of hope."**

*Aaron Henry*

Born to sharecroppers in Dublin, Mississippi, Aaron Henry was a civil rights activist and politician for most of his life. After attending Xavier University of Louisiana and opening a drugstore in Clarksdale, he co-founded, with several others, the Regional Council of Negro Leadership (RCNL). He started the Mississippi Freedom Democratic Party and organized a boycott of discriminatory Clarksdale stores. In 1982 he was elected to the Mississippi House of Representatives and held his seat until 1996.

**Photograph** Aaron Henry, chair of the Mississippi Freedom Democratic Party delegation, speaks before the Credentials Committee at the
Democratic National Convention, Atlantic City, New Jersey, August 1964
Photo by Buyenlarge/Getty Images

# WILLIAM WINTER

## GOVERNOR, EDUCATION REFORMER, RECONCILER

In 1947, while still in law school, William Winter was elected to the Mississippi House of Representatives. He later served as the 58th Governor of Mississippi from 1980 to 1984. Winter was an early proponent of public education and racial reconciliation, as well as historic preservation. As governor, Winter lead the charge for publicly-funded primary education. His governance echoed his belief that all people, regardless of race or class, should be entitled to the same rights that the most privileged enjoy.

Unlike most public figures, Winter wrote all of his own speeches. His 2006 book, *The Measure of Our Days: Writings of William F. Winter* (with Andy Mullins) presented a collection of the governor's most thoughtful writings on his home state, the South, and America in general.

In March 2008, he was given the Profile in Courage Award by the John F. Kennedy Presidential Library and Museum for his work advancing education and racial reconciliation. The William Winter Institute for Racial Reconciliation on the University of Mississippi's Oxford campus is named in his honor.

**Photograph** courtesy The University of Mississippi

# MYRLIE EVERS-WILLIAMS
## CIVIL RIGHTS ACTIVIST

**"We knew the job was dangerous."**
*Myrlie Evers-Williams*

Myrlie Evers met her husband, Medgar, when they were students at Alcorn A & M College. After Medgar Evers' death, Evers-Williams enrolled at Pomona College in California and graduated in 1968 with a degree in sociology.

Evers-Williams was appointed chairperson of the NAACP (she served from 1995 to 1998). She is credited with spearheading the operations that restored the association to its original status as the premier civil rights organization in America.

She is the author of *For Us, the Living* (1967) and *Watch Me Fly: What I Learned On the Way to Becoming the Woman I Was Meant to Be* (1999). In the bestseller, *I Dream A World: Black Women Who Changed America*, Evers-Williams wrote that she "greets today and the future with open arms."

Whoopi Goldberg played Evers-Williams in the film *Ghosts of Mississippi*.

**Photograph** NAACP Chairman Myrlie Evers-Williams speaks onstage during the 41st NAACP Image awards held in Los Angeles, California. Photo by Michael Caulfield/WireImage

# FLORENCE MARS

PHOTOGRAPHER, CIVIL RIGHTS ACTIVIST

**"She saw, she heard, she felt, and through her own involvement she bore witness to qualities of courage and goodwill that all but evaporated in the climate of passion that flowed from an unreasoning fear of change."**

*Turner Catledge, former editor of the* New York Times

Barely five feet tall, Florence Mars more than made up in confidence and determination what she lacked in height. A Neshoba County resident, Mars was a freelance photographer who consistently spoke out against racism and the Ku Klux Klan, unafraid of the repercussions from other Southerners. Locals boycotted her cattleyard and she was forced to resign as a Sunday School teacher. Undeterred, Mars decided to write about the murders of Andrew Goodman, James Earl Chaney and Michael Schwerner in her book *Witness in Philadelphia*, "in an effort to reconcile her personal outrage and shame for what occurred with some understanding of why it happened." Revered as a strong civil rights activist, Florence Mars passed away at her home in 2006.

**Photograph** courtesy Dawn Lea Mars Chalmers

# DUNCAN GRAY, JR.

RELIGIOUS LEADER

**"The first thing we can do is to face up to our own guilt in the situation…We are responsible for the moral and political climate in our state which made such a tragedy possible…The things that we have 'left undone that we ought to have done' should bother us every bit as much as the 'things which we have done that we ought not to have done.'"**

*From a sermon on Oct. 7, 1962, a week after the riots at Ole Miss*

Reverend Duncan Gray, Jr. was a light in the darkness when it came to Southern race relations in the 1950s and 60s. When James Meredith was enrolling at Ole Miss, and riots broke out on the campus, Rev. Gray was in the middle of the crowd, pleading with rioters to end the violence. Even though he didn't stop the riots, he was never disheartened, and always stood for integration.

As the author of "The Church Considers the Supreme Court's Decision," written after Brown v. Board of Education declared "separate but equal" to be unconstitutional, Rev. Gray used biblical references to support his stance that racism is a sin, and that the church should always stand for equal treatment of human beings. He wrote, "Man, be he white or black, is made in the image of God."

Later elected as Bishop of the Episcopal Diocese of Mississippi, a position he held for twenty years, Rev. Gray continues to support ending racism in the South.

**Photograph** courtesy Episcopal Diocese of Mississippi

# CHARLES EVERS

**"I'd rather be dead and in heaven than afraid to do what I think is right."**

*Charles Evers*

When he served in the Army, Charles Evers fell in love with a Filipino woman but knew he could not return to Mississippi with her because of their differing skin colors. He returned to Mississippi and began working for civil rights, becoming an active member in the Regional Council of Negro Leadership (started by Mississippian Aaron Henry). He continued to work for civil rights after the murder of his brother and fellow activist, Medgar Evers, and eventually became the first African-American since Reconstruction to be elected as a Mississippi town mayor, in Fayette. He ran for governor in 1971 and U.S. Senate in 1978 as an independent, and continues to be outspoken about civil rights. He published his autobiography, *Have No Fear: The Charles Evers Story*, in 1996.

**Photograph:** Evers during his campaign as Democratic candidate for mayor. Photo by Charles Bonnay/Time Life Pictures

# MARTHA BERGMARK
## FOUNDER, MISSISSIPPI CENTER FOR JUSTICE

Martha Bergmark's parents were active in the Mississippi civil rights movement in the 1950s. Bergmark followed their lead while a student at Murrah High in the 1960s. She left Mississippi for Oberlin College in Ohio and then went on to the University of Michigan Law School. Returning to Mississippi, she opened a civil rights practice in Hattiesburg and later was director of the indigent legal services office there. Bergmark then moved to Washington, DC and became a national leader in provision of legal services for the poor. In 2003, she left it all to establish the Mississippi Center for Justice — a non-profit law firm dedicated to racial and economic justice. Bergmark and the staff at the Mississippi Center for Justice work every day for equal justice under the law. Bergmark said, "As long as there are some who can't afford justice, then we can't have justice for all."

Rights for juveniles, affordable housing, predatory lending, access to health care — Bergmark leads a team that confronts these seemingly intractable problems. They were one of the first groups to mobilize resources to help provide legal services for victims of Hurricane Katrina.

**Photograph** courtesy Mississippi Center for Justice

# ROBERT MCDUFF

ATTORNEY

Growing up in Hattiesburg during the civil rights movement, Rob McDuff became interested in civil rights and was intrigued by the drama of the courtroom. While at Millsaps College, he worked part-time for a civil rights law office on Farish Street. After graduating from Harvard Law School, he worked in a variety of public interest law jobs in Memphis, Oxford, and Washington, DC, before returning south to open his own civil rights and criminal defense practice in Jackson.

Much of his work has involved redistricting challenges to discriminatory election districts throughout the country. In one of his first cases, McDuff was part of the team that filed the lawsuit leading to the election of the first black member of Congress in Mississippi since Reconstruction. Over his career, he has handled a variety of cases involving police misconduct, jail conditions, free speech, indigent defense funding, reproductive freedom, school prayer, and discrimination in employment and housing.

McDuff's courtroom victories include the successful defense of Mississippi Supreme Court justice Oliver Diaz against federal criminal charges in two separate trials, and McDuff has helped to obtain the release of a number of innocent prisoners in Mississippi and Louisiana. As one of the defense lawyers in the Jena 6 case, he helped negotiate a resolution leading to the expungement of the controversial charges that had been brought against several Louisiana teenagers and had led to nationwide protests. His practice spans all levels of the court system, including four cases that he argued in the United States Supreme Court. His work has been recognized by a number of awards, including the 2009 Advocacy Award of the National NAACP and the Pro Bono Service Award of the International Human Rights Law Group.

**Photograph** by Jackson Free Press

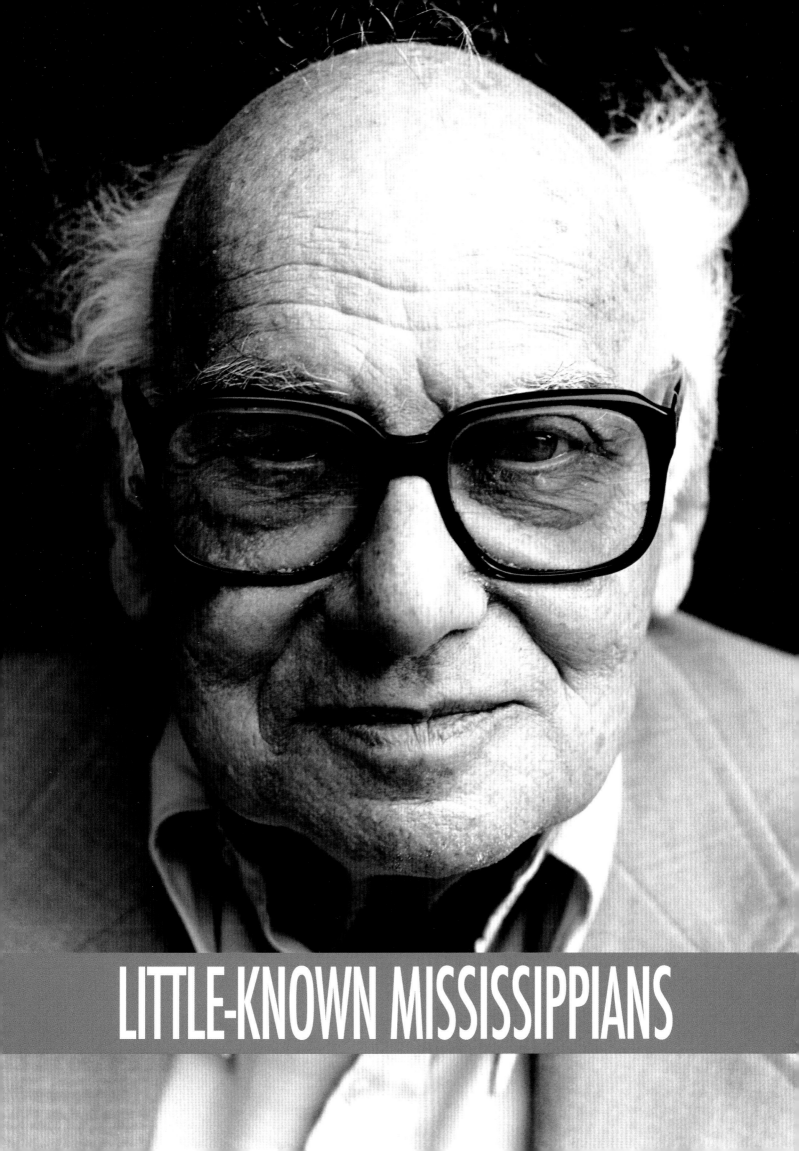

LITTLE-KNOWN MISSISSIPPIANS

# WYATT COOPER

WRITER, ACTOR, SOCIALITE

**"In my sons' youth, their promise, their possibilities, my stake in immortality is invested."**

*Wyatt Cooper, from his memoir,* Families: A Memoir and a Celebration

Quitman, Mississippi native Wyatt Cooper moved to New York City in his twenties to pursue acting. Though he appeared in a number of Broadway plays and small television series (he also appeared as "Tommy" in the 1961 film *Sanctuary*), Cooper's gift was writing. He wrote the television screenplay for *The Chapman Report*, and he collaborated with Truman Capote on the screenplay for *The Glass House*. He also wrote for *Esquire*.

In 1963, he married socialite Gloria Vanderbilt (they were a staple on the national "best dressed" list). The couple had two sons — one of whom is Anderson Cooper, the CNN anchor.

**Photograph** of Wyatt Cooper and Gloria Vanderbilt at a Charlie Chaplin tribute. Photo by Ron Galella/WireImage

# OSEOLA MCCARTY

PHILANTHROPIST

**"I don't know that I have ever been as touched by a gift to the university as I am by this one."**

*Aubrey Lucas, President, USM*

Oseola McCarty was just in sixth grade when she left school to care for an ailing relative. For three generations, Hattiesburg families hired McCarty to handle their laundry. Little did they know, someday she was going to do something very important with their money.

Each week, she invested a portion of her earnings at her local bank. When she turned 87, arthritis forced her to put down her iron and she decided it was time to do something with all that cash. After giving some to the church and some to family members, she donated the rest — all $150,000 of it — to The University of Southern Mississippi. "I just want the scholarship to go to some child who needs it, to whoever is not able to help their children," McCarty said. "I'm too old to get an education, but they can."

**Photograph** Oseola McCarty shares a laugh with President Bill Clinton after receiving a Presidential Medal of Honor.
Photo by Terry Ashe/*Time Life* Pictures

# MINNIE COX

TRAILBLAZER

In 1891, Minnie Cox was appointed postmaster in Indianola, Mississippi. Many historians believe she was the first African-American female postmaster in the United States. The Indianola postmaster position was a highly respected, lucrative post ($1,100 annually). Cox was efficient and dedicated, but many white citizens of Indianola called for her removal (including a newspaper editor from Greenwood who hoped to take her place).

Cox refused to step down even amidst threats of physical violence. Rather than appoint a replacement, President Theodore Roosevelt suspended the Indianola post office, re-routed the town's mail and announced that the local branch would not be reopened until Cox could resume her duties.

The controversy surrounding Cox's position made news across the country. It was debated for four hours on the United States Senate floor. The atmosphere eventually became so hostile that, in 1903, Mrs. Cox left Indianola for her own safety.

**Photograph** courtesy *The Enterprise-Tocsin*

# RICHARD RAGAN

UNITED NATIONS REPRESENTATIVE

During a stint on the National Security Council while serving in the Clinton administration, Cleveland native Richard Ragan's curiosity was piqued. He noticed the United Nations' World Food Program was the most "can do" of all the UN agencies. So Ragan joined the team. He was first stationed in China where he managed the UN response to the devastating 1998 Yangtze River flood that affected over 180 million people. He followed as the representative in Zambia during the drought in southern Africa. Then he served as UN boss in North Korea. For two years Ragan was the only American to live (with permission) in the secretive country. Wearing his signature baseball cap and long hair, Ragan zipped around Pyongyang on a motorcycle while working to feed the country's six million malnourished people. He now serves as the World Food Program Country Representative in Nepal, where he lives with his wife and children. In his free time Ragan guides heliskiing trips in the world's highest mountain range.

**Photograph:** Richard Ragan (left) in Nepal receiving gifts from children who just discovered he had supplied them food for the last year.

# BURNITA SHELTON MATTHEWS

LAWYER, ACTIVIST, JUDGE

Burnita Shelton Matthews, a Hazlehurst native, was the first woman appointed to serve as a U.S. District Judge. Sent to a conservatory by her father (he thought she should earn a living teaching music), she instead enrolled in law school. After graduation, she passed the District of Columbia bar exam, but the DC bar association returned her application and dues check.

Matthews and several other female attorneys formed their own professional associations — the Woman's Bar Association of the District of Columbia and the National Association of Women Lawyers.

In 1948, President Harry S. Truman named Matthews to the U.S. District Court for the District of Columbia. She was confirmed by the United States Senate the following year. Matthews heard several newsworthy cases, including the 1956 bribery trial of Jimmy Hoffa. She served until her death in 1988.

**Photograph** courtesy Mississippi Department of Archives and History

# MILTON BABBITT

COMPOSER

Known as a composer and music theorist, Milton Babbitt began his lifelong career in music when he took up the violin at age 4. Raised in Jackson, he was writing his own arrangements of popular songs at age seven and at 13, he won a local songwriting contest. The recipient of one of Princeton's first MFA degrees in 1942, Babbitt taught at both Princeton and Juilliard, where he taught notable students such as Stephen Sondheim, the musical theater composer, and Stanley Jordan, the jazz guitarist. From 1985 until his death in 2011, Babbitt was the chairman of the BMI Student Composer Awards, always encouraging young musicians to pursue their dreams and polish their talents.

**Photograph** by Lebrecht Music & Arts

# JONATHAN MURRAY

REALITY TELEVISION CREATOR

Reality television was created by a Mississippian. When Gulfport native Jonathan Murray was paired with Mary-Ellis Bunim to write a soap opera for MTV, they realized the show would be too expensive. So they decided to try something else: an unscripted soap opera. The result was *Real World*. The two founded Bunim/Murray productions, and created other reality shows such as *Road Rules*, *Making the Band* and *The Real World/Road Rules Challenge*.

**Photograph** Jonathan Murray poses for a portrait during the 2008 Toronto International Film Festival. Photo by Matt Carr/Getty Images

# RUSS DALLEN

EDITOR & PUBLISHER

President and Editor-in-Chief of the *Latin American Herald Tribune* since January of 2008, Russ Dallen has worked and written for publications all over the world. Getting his start as a Gulfport, Mississippi paperboy at age 13, he studied economics, political science, law, international affairs and international law at the Universities of Oxford, Columbia, Nottingham, and Mississippi. *The Common Market Law Review*, Europe's leading legal journal, named his Masters Thesis Article of the Year. He has published articles and editorials in *Newsweek, The Daily Telegraph, The Oxford Eagle* and *The Daily Herald*. Constantly trying to encourage young students, he is currently a member of the Board of Directors of the Venezuelan American Friendship Association, which provides scholarships to worthy Venezuelan students.

**Photograph** courtesy *Latin American Herald Tribune*

# RUBY ELZY

SINGER

Though born into poverty in Pontotoc, Mississippi, Ruby Elzy dreamed of a career on the stage. She first sang publicly at age four and was later heard singing by a visiting professor in Mississippi, who then arranged for her to study music at Ohio State University. Later she earned a Rosenwald Fellowship and enrolled at Juilliard. She entertained Eleanor Roosevelt at the White House, she appeared opposite Bing Crosby in *Birth of the Blues*, and she created the role of Serena in the original production of *Porgy and Bess*. She was set to debut at the Met (some ten years before Leontyne Price did) when, undergoing routine surgery, she died at age 35. Though often overlooked in history, Elzy paved the way for African American singers like Price, Jessye Norman, and others.

**Photograph** courtesy David Weaver, author of *Elzy, Black Diva of the Thirties*

# JOHN C. ROBINSON

### THE BROWN CONDOR

John C. Robinson saw his first plane in Gulfport, Mississippi. He dreamed of one day flying a plane. When Italy invaded Ethiopia in 1935, Robinson volunteered to join the Ethiopian defense. He fulfilled his dream of becoming a pilot and gained fame as an aviation pioneer. Robinson was appointed by Emperor Haile Selassie to command the Imperial Ethiopian Air Corps during the brutal Italo-Ethiopian War of 1935. He was very likely the first American to engage in armed conflict against fascism. He went on to teach the first generation of Ethiopian pilots, many of whom would join the first African airline company, Ethiopian Airlines. He remained in Ethiopia until his death in 1954.

 The story of John Robinson was overshadowed by the Spanish Civil War and lost in the chaos of World War II. It was rediscovered by Gulfport author Thomas E. Simmons in the narrative biography *The Brown Condor*. A bronze bust of Col. Robinson now resides in the Gulfport-Biloxi Airport Terminal.

**Photograph** courtesy Thomas Simmons

# TENA CLARK

COMPOSER, LYRICIST, PRODUCER

**"I have to feel something to write it."**

*Tena Clark*

What do Aretha Franklin and President Obama share? The musical expertise of Mississippian Tena Clark. Clark, the founder and CEO of DMI Music, programs music for Air Force One. She also produced the Queen of Soul's last album.

Beginning at the age of five, Clark traveled with her mother, a songwriter in the Big Band era, to New Orleans. Clark performed her first professional gig — at age 15 — playing drums at the Roosevelt Hotel. Since then, she has penned country music hits, collaborated on award-winning movie soundtracks, written for hit television series and won a Grammy. And still Clark had time to create the iconic McDonald's campaign, "Have you had your break today?"

One of the rare female producers in the music industry, Clark was recently named "Entrepreneur of the Year" by the Committee of 200.

Her most recent venture, *Twist: An American Musical*, played to rave reviews in Atlanta and Los Angeles — and some crtics insist it's Broadway bound. Clark served as composer, lyricist and producer.

If the past 13 years are any indication, we'll be hearing a lot more from Tena Clark.

# ELIZABETH DOLLARHIDE

WRITER, PRODUCER

Elizabeth Dollarhide's first film job was working with the crew of *The Gun in Betty Lou's Handbag*, which was shot on location in her hometown of Oxford. She worked her way up through the industry and when she relocated to Los Angeles, she was hired by filmmaker Lawrence Kasdan. She worked with Kasdan on development, casting and production. After producing Kasdan's film *Dreamcatcher*, she segued into writing and producing DVD documentaries for *Cinderalla Man*, *Parenthood*, *Flags of Our Fathers*, *Letters from Iwo Jima*, among others, as well as an HBO special on *Cinderella Man*. Dollarhide now lives in Taylor, Mississippi. She is writing and producing an adaptation of a novel, scheduled to shoot in France. She recently produced a website designed to sell Oxford as an ideal filming location. Dollarhide served as associate editor of photography of this edition of *Mississippians*.

**Photograph** by Paul Black

# LAWRENCE "RABBIT" KENNEDY

WAR HERO

Command Sergeant Major Lawrence E. Kennedy, from Amory, is the most decorated soldier in the history of the U.S. Army. He served in the Vietnam War and wears four Legions of Merit and 34 Air Medals.

He was inducted into the Army Aviation Hall of Fame in 1977.

# COL. PRENTISS INGRAHAM

PROLIFIC WRITER

A Confederate Colonel from Natchez, Prentiss Ingraham was most well-known for his Buffalo Bill series of books. To say that Ingraham was prolific is a vast understatement. He claimed to have written over 600 novels and 400 novellas (many under pen names).

**Photograph** Rare photography of Col. Prentis Ingraham (top) posing with Buffalo Bill (circa 1880).
Photo courtesy Special Collections, University of Mississippi Libraries

# VAN DYKE PARKS

MUSICIAN

Composer, arranger, producer, musician, singer and author, Van Dyke Parks began his early career as a child actor, working in film and television, including a movie with Grace Kelly and a recurring role in Jackie Gleason's *The Honeymooners*. After switching to a musical career and studying at the Carnegie Institute, the Hattiesburg native performed on The Byrds' album *Fifth Dimension* and began an ill-fated collaboration with Brian Wilson of the Beach Boys on *Smile*. After *Smile* was shelved, many of the songs were later released on *Smiley Smile*, *Surf's Up*, and *Sunflower*. Wilson and Parks rerecorded the *Smile* album in 2004. Parks' first solo album *Song Cycle* was critically acclaimed and in 1972 he produced *Discover America*, his take on calypso music. His music is known for its eclecticism, imagery and inspiration. Artists he has performed with, produced, or arranged are a veritable who's who list of pop music, from U2 to Ry Cooder to Randy Newman and Ringo Starr.

**Photograph** courtesy Michael Ochs Archive

# PEGGY DOW

ACTOR

Peggy Dow was born Margaret Josephine Varnadow in Columbia, Mississippi. After a brief stint in modeling and radio, Peggy's beauty and stage presence attracted a Hollywood agent who signed her to Universal Studios. Unlike most young starlets, Peggy never acted in bit parts. She began her acting career at the top — she starred as the leading lady in two feature-length films within the first year of her contract. Without a doubt Peggy's most memorable role was that of Nurse Kelly in the James Stewart hit *Harvey*. She retired from acting in 1951 when she married her husband Walter Helmerich, after only three years of acting.

**Photograph** by by Ralph Crane/Time Life Pictures

# KEITH THIBODEAUX
CHILD ACTOR

Keith Thibodeaux starred in one of the most-watched television shows of the 1950s, *I Love Lucy*. Yet he could not be recognized as that character today. Thibodeaux played the son of Lucy and Ricky Ricardo, Little Ricky. After acting alongside Hollywood greats Lucille Ball and Desi Arnaz, Thibodeaux joined a rock band called David and the Giants. They toured around the south for over 20 years and had several regional hits. In 1976, he married a ballet dancer and only three years later moved to Jackson, Mississippi, where he now resides.

**Photograph** Desi Arnaz, Lucille Ball, Keith Thibodeaux, Vivian Vance and William Frawley in a group studio portrait for *I Love Lucy*.
Silver Screen Collection

# EDDIE HODGES

CHILD ACTOR

Eddie Hodges was born in Hattiesburg in 1947 — by 1957, at the age of 10, he was performing in his first Broadway production, The Music Man. He made his big-screen debut two years later in *A Hole in the Head*, in which he sang a duet with Frank Sinatra called "High Hopes." He starred as Huckleberry Finn in Michael Curtis's *The Adventures of Huckleberry Finn* (1960). Hodges guest starred in several television shows during his career, including *Bonanza*, *Gunsmoke*, *The Dick van Dyke Show*, and *What's My Line?* After serving in the Vietnam War, Hodges gave up on show business and returned to Mississippi to receive his degree from The University of Southern Mississippi.

**Photograph** Eddie Hodges plays Huck Finn in *The Adventures of Huckleberry Finn*. Photo by Grey Villet/*Time Life* Pictures

# LILLIAN SHEDD MCMURRY

MUSIC PRODUCER

Lillian Shedd McMurry, from Purvis, Mississippi, discovered blues music after she married. Digging through her husband's record collection, she found inspiration in the old blues recordings and decided to open a recording studio of her own. Trumpet Records opened in 1950 and there McMurry recorded Elmore James and Aleck "Rice" Miller (aka Sonny Boy Williamson), among others. Even though financial problems caused Trumpet Records to close just five years after opening, McMurry's contributions were acknowledged with her induction into the Blues Hall of Fame in 1998, and in 2007 a historical marker was placed at the location of the old studio.

**Photograph** by Bill Ferris

# JEFF HAMMOND

RETIRED GENERAL

Major General (Retired) Jeff Hammond received his commission as an Army Officer upon graduation from the University of Southern Mississippi in 1978. His military career spanned 32 years. Hammond's service included command positions as a Battery, Battalion, and Brigade Commander, and most recently as Commanding General, 4th Infantry Division as Commanding General, Multi-National Division Baghdad in Iraq.

During the operational deployment in Iraq, his more than 28,000 soldiers achieved unprecedented battlefield success in protecting the people of Iraq and establishing long term peace and stability. They decreased violence by 80 percent, captured more than 3,700 terrorists, created over 50,000 jobs, rebuilt 210 schools/medical clinics and conducted the first ever non-violent democratic Provincial Election.

Hammond was elected into the USM Sports Hall of Fame and Alumni Hall of Fame. His military decorations include two awards of the Distinguished Service Medal, three awards of the Bronze Star Medal and two awards of the Combat Action Badge. But Hammond is quick to tell you his greatest achievement is being a husband and father.

# JACK GREGORY

EARLY BLIND SIDER

Okolona native E. J. "Jack" Gregory, Jr. was one of the first free agents in professional football. While a player with the New York Giants his career as a defensive end blossomed. Defensive coordinator (and eventual Giant Head coach) Bill Arnsparger designed the "rover position" around Gregory because of his ability to pressure the quarterback. In the rover position Gregory led the league in quarterback sacks. Gregory was the inspiration for the new defensive scheme, later made famous by Lawrence Taylor as detailed in *The Blind Side*.

**Photograph** courtesy the Gregory family

# DEACON JONES

DEFENSIVE END

Deacon Jones played football for one season at South Carolina State. After his first year, the school revoked Jones' scholarship because they learned he was a part of a civil rights movement.

One of the assistant football coaches at South Carolina State was leaving to coach at Mississippi Vocational (Mississippi Valley State University) and told Jones he would try to get him a scholarship.

Jones, who specialized in quarterback sacks and claimed to have coined the term, played his last year of college football for a Mississippi school. Nicknamed the "Secretary of Defense," Jones is considered one of the greatest defensive players in the history of the NFL.

**Photograph** by Walter Iooss Jr. /Sports Illustrated

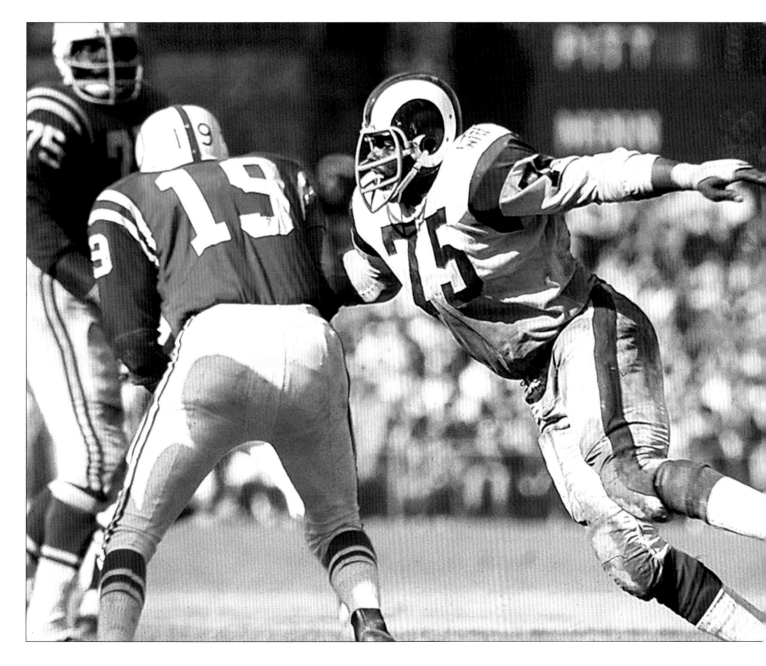

# BLANCHE COLTON WILLIAMS

O. HENRY AWARD FOUNDER, TRAILBLAZER

Considered a genius by many of her teachers, Blanche Colton Williams entered college at age 15, graduating with honors at 19. Originally from Kosciusko, she taught at schools throughout Mississippi, and was the recipient of a fellowship that allowed her to continue learning at Columbia University. The first woman allowed to use the Oxford English Library, she was also the first chairman and one of the founders of the O. Henry Memorial Award.

**Photograph** courtesy of Mississippi University for Women

# TIG NOTARO

COMEDIAN

**"Notaro has an unassuming onstage style that's immediately disarming, and the unrushed storytelling of *Good One* unfolds like a good hang."**

*AV Club*

Stand-up comedian Tig Notaro was born in Jackson and raised in Pass Christian. After dropping out of high school, she worked in the music industry until her job took her to Los Angeles and she attempted stand-up comedy for the first time. Since then, she appeared on 2006's *Last Comic Standing* and has been featured on *Comedy Central Presents* and *The Sarah Silverman Program*. In 2011, she released her debut comedy album, *Good One*.

**Photograph** Tig Notaro on stage during Bonnaroo 2011 at The Comedy Theatre, Manchester, Tennessee.
Photo by FilmMagic

# RICKY STENHOUSE, JR.

NASCAR DRIVER

The 2010 NASCAR Nationwide Rookie of the Year, Olive Branch-native Ricky Stenhouse, Jr. began racing go-karts at age six. In 2006, he was the National Sprint Car Hall of Fame Driver Poll Wild Card title winner in both the 360 and 410 winged sprint car divisions. He currently drives the 6 Blackwell Angus Beef Ford Fusion for Roush Fenway Racing in the NASCAR Nationwide Series. In 2011, at age 23, he made his Cup Series debut at the Coca-Cola 600, and finished 11th in the Wood Brothers Racing entry.

**Photograph** by Ronald C. Modra/Sports Imagery

# DENT MAY

MUSICIAN

Dent May has pop music's version of attention deficit disorder. Between his 2009 debut LP of ukulele tunes on Paw Tracks, a mysterious unfinished psych-country rock opera *Cowboy Maloney's Electric City*, dance recordings under the Dent Sweat moniker, and countless other musical personas, Dent has covered a lot of ground. A lifelong Mississippi resident (Dent grew up in Jackson but now calls Oxford home), he founded the Cats Purring collective (which includes Dead Gaze, Flight, and Bass Drum of Death) and throws notorious DIY shows at his home at the Cats Purring Dude Ranch. Dent just put the finishing touches on his new studio album *Hits Incorporated* where he's tapping into influences ranging from The Zombies to Teddy Riley to Aaliyah. His latest release is a 7" single on *Forest Family* featuring the songs "That Feeling" and "Eastover Wives," the latter of which *Transparent* calls "a mischievous ode to wayward babes that sees Dent's dangerously smooth croon sashaying on a mirrorball-lit dancefloor of fruity saxophone trills, cinematic synth strings and horny, whiteboy funk guitars."

**Photograph** courtesy Dent May

# RICKY ROBERTSON

HIGH JUMPER

In 2008, as a Hernando High School track star, Ricky Robertson had the highest jump in the nation: seven feet three inches. The leap also set a new Mississippi high school record.

At Ole Miss, Robertson was named a U.S. Track & Field All-American. He was named All-SEC first team and SEC All-Freshman team in the high jump. He was also selected as SEC Outdoor Freshman Field Athlete of the Year. If that weren't enough, as a freshman he won the SEC Championship in the high jump with a leap of seven feet, two-and-a-half inches. Robertson went on to place fifth in the nation as a freshman.

Keep your eye on Robertson. This Hernando native is going to reach new heights.

**Photograph** courtesy The University of Mississippi

# SAM KENDRICKS

POLE VAULTER

Oxford's Sam Kendricks set a new, all-time Mississippi pole vault record in 2011 with a mark of 17 feet. The former record was just under 16 feet. If that weren't impressive enough, Kendricks broke meet records in all ten of his high school track events. He was recently named the Gatorade Mississippi Boys Athlete of the Year.

Kendricks also keeps high marks in the classroom. He gradated from high school with a 3.70 GPA. In February of 2011, Kendricks signed with the track team at Ole Miss.

**Photograph** by Bruce Newman

# SARAH FRANCES HARDY

ARTIST, WRITER

Artist and writer Sarah Frances Hardy was raised in Jackson, Mississippi. She attended Davidson College as a fine arts major and studied for two summers at Parsons School of Design in New York and Paris. She received a law degree from the University of Mississippi School of Law but decided to paint and write full time instead. She has exhibited work in galleries in the Southeast as well as New York.

Hardy's third grade teacher dubbed her "Miss Creativity" and predicted that she would someday make it onto the bookstore shelves. Her first, highly-anticipated children's book, *Puzzled by Pink*, will be published in 2012 by Viking Children's Books. She currently lives in Oxford and is working on another picture book, as well as a middle grade novel set in the South.

**Photograph** by Bella Vie Photograph

# WHITNEY MILLER

CHEF, AUTHOR

Seven minutes. That's how long Whitney Miller had to cook her second piece of chicken, after dropping the first, on the finale of *MasterChef*. She not only cooked the chicken to perfection, she won the whole competition. Only 23 years old, Miller has recently published her first cookbook, *Modern Hospitality: Simple Recipes with Southern Charm*.

# DEXTER MCCLUSTER

NFL PLAYER

Dexter McCluster dazzled Ole Miss fans for four years in Oxford. Now, Kansas City fans will take notice whenever he touches the ball. In 2010, McCluster signed a $5.15 million, 4-year contract with the Chiefs. During pre-season drills, speedy McCluster literally ran out of his shoes . . . twice. He scored his first NFL touchdown in his debut game on a 94-yard punt return against the San Diego Chargers. The return was the longest punt return in Chiefs history.

If McCluster, who stands 5' 8" tall and weighs 172 lbs, can stay healthy, he might just be an NFL superstar.

**Photograph** by Bruce Newman

# MARCUS DUPREE

EX-FOOTBALL PLAYER

The heartbreaking career of Marcus Dupree is well known by most Mississippians. However, Dupree is going through a renaissance.

The ESPN documentary titled *The Best That Never Was* — directed by Jonathan Hock as part of the *30 for 30* series — has sparked renewed interest in Dupree.

After he was released by the Los Angeles Rams in 1992, he performed as a professional wrestler. Later he managed a sports bar and worked as a casino greeter. But now, Dupree is on the speakers circuit. He's contemplating movie deals. He's even considering writing a memoir that would pick up where Willie Morris' *The Courting of Marcus Dupree* left off.

Mississippians were certain Marcus Dupree would hit the big time through football. Perhaps the real story is about how he lived through failure. Keep an eye on Dupree.

**Photograph** Marcus Dupree scores a touchdown vs Nebraska in1982. Photo by Rich Clarkson/Sports Illustrated

# WRIGHT THOMPSON
JOURNALIST, WRITER

Clarksdale native Wright Thompson has every sports fan's dream job. He writes for ESPN. And he's good at it.

Thompson writes long-form narrative for ESPN.com and *ESPN The Magazine*. He reports from all corners of the United States — as well as five continents. He has access to sports figures most of us only dream about meeting. Thompson also reports for *E:60* and *Outside the Lines*, and contributes stories (written and recorded) for *SportsCenter*, the Masters and British Open coverage, *College Gameday*, *NFL Sunday Countdown* and other ESPN platforms and show.

Thompson's work has been selected six times for Houghton-Mifflin's *Best American Sports Writing* anthology. He's won an Emmy, the Edward R. Murrow Award and the National Headliner Award.

Despite winning just about every award possible in the sports reportage world, Thompson is just getting started. His work is lauded by other writers. And they sense bigger projects over the horizon. Thompson seems to be following the footsteps of another great Southern journalist, Rick Bragg. And that path leads straight into the world of literature.

**Photograph** Wright Thompson in a Cuban dugout. Photo by ESPN.

# MICHAEL GRIMM

SINGER

After singing at a wedding when he was 11, Michael Grimm was invited to sing at a local bar... as long as he brought a legal guardian with him. Raised in Waveland, Mississippi by his piano-playing grandmother, Grimm loved music from an early age. After performing in Las Vegas for a while, Grimm auditioned for *America's Got Talent* in 2010 and ended up winning the competition. With a musical style he refers to as "soulful Americana," Grimm released his self-titled debut album in 2011.

# LACEY CHABERT

ACTOR

Born and raised in Purvis, Mississippi, Lacey Chabert has been performing for just about her entire life. A talented violinist as well as actress and singer, she appeared on *Star Search* in 1991 and then played young Cosette (and occasionally, the male character of Gavroche) in Broadway's *Les Miserables* for two years. Chabert became well known to TV audiences as Claudia on *Party of Five* and as the voice of Eliza on *The Wild Thornberrys*. Chabert regained popularity as an adult when she played the insecure and always gossiping Gretchen Wieners in *Mean Girls*.

**Photograph** Lacey Chabert at *The Wild Thornberrys* premiere. Photo by Gregg DeGuire/WireImage

# AUSTIN EVANS & RICHARD PATRICK

CATHEAD VODKA FOUNDERS

Now one year old, Cathead Vodka has already become a success story in Mississippi. The first to pass the test for operating a Mississippi distillery, Austin Evans and Richard Patrick met at the University of Alabama as small business management majors. When they decided to start their own business, they hearkened to Mississippi's blues history to find their name: "Back in the day, blues musicians were referred to as 'cats,'" Evans said.

Today, Cathead can be found in seven states. The founders are committed to supporting regional artists and musicians. Depending on where you buy your product, $1 of every 750 ml bottle goes to a local charity. In Evans' home state of Mississippi, the money supports the Yoknapatawpha Arts Council.

# CARTER MYERS

ENTREPRENEUR

**"You watch students with cameras, have them walk through metal detectors, but at some point we have to tell students, 'it is your school, your climate, you need to step up and take responsibility for it.'"**

*Carter Myers*

Carter Myers is using technology to revolutionize communication between students, teachers and counselors in schools. The president of AnComm, Myers has been instrumental in creating the first anonymous texting service that allows students to get in touch with counselors without fear of getting in trouble, or suffering embarrassment or retaliation from other students. The service has been used to address abuse, bullying, sexual harassment, suicide, weapons in school, rape, depression and many other issues that teens often face.

AnComm was founded in 2005 when it purchased the nonprofit Safety Organization for Schools, and has created programs such as "Talk About It," which has played a central role in preventing at least three suicides in Mississippi and Texas schools, and the Global Alert™ Emergency Notification Service, which allows schools to send real-time messages to students in times of danger. AnComm is expanding, with corporate headquarters in Oxford, Mississippi, and offices in Houston, Texas, and today, some 400 schools in 19 states are implementing these programs. Myers feels that schools need to embrace technology instead of banning it, saying, "Schools in the beginning had the attitude of, 'Let's keep technology away from students.' But our belief was why not tap into this and channel it."

**Photograph** by Scott Burton

# COLORFUL CHARACTERS

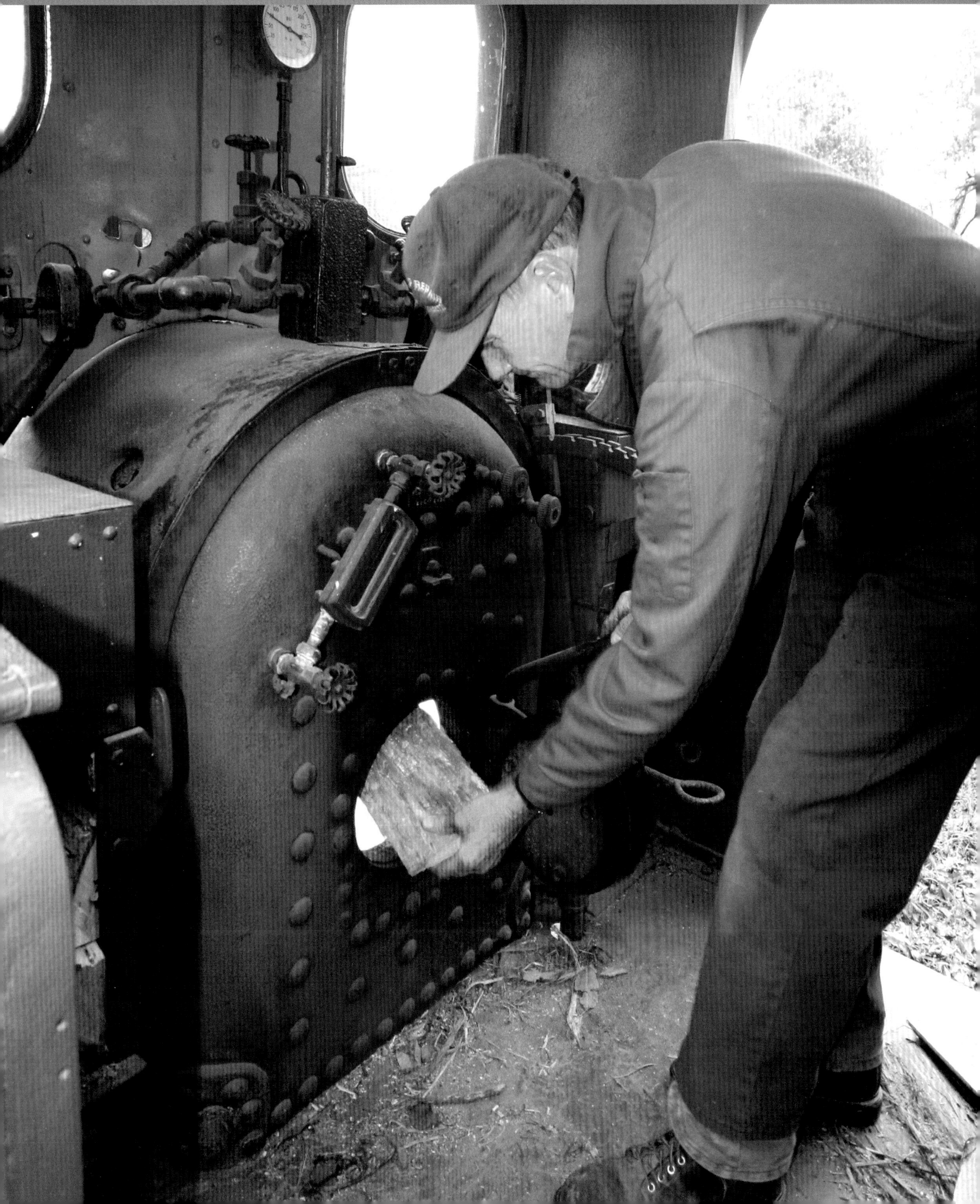

# NOAH "SOGGY" SWEAT
ATTORNEY

Judge Noah "Soggy" Sweat was many things: a judge, a law professor, a Mississippi state representative, and the founder of the Mississippi Judicial College of the University of Mississippi Law Center.

But he is best known (and most often imitated) for a speech he delivered in 1952 on the floor of the Mississippi state legislature on the subject of prohibition. It is known as: "The Whiskey Speech."

## THE WHISKEY SPEECH

My friends,

I had not intended to discuss this controversial subject at this particular time. However, I want you to know that I do not shun controversy. On the contrary, I will take a stand on any issue at any time, regardless of how fraught with controversy it might be. You have asked me how I feel about whiskey. All right, here is how I feel about whiskey.

If when you say whiskey you mean the devil's brew, the poison scourge, the bloody monster that defiles innocence, dethrones reason, destroys the home, creates misery and poverty, yea, literally takes the bread from the mouths of little children; if you mean the evil drink that topples the Christian man and woman from the pinnacle of righteous, gracious living into the bottomless pit of degradation, and despair, and shame and helplessness, and hopelessness, then certainly I am against it.

But . . .

If when you say whiskey you mean the oil of conversation, the philosophic wine, the ale that is consumed when good fellows get together that puts a song in their hearts and laughter on their lips and the warm glow of contentment in their eyes; if you mean Christmas cheer; if you mean the stimulating drink that puts the spring in the old gentleman's step on a frosty, crispy morning; if you mean the drink which enables a man to magnify his joy, and his happiness, and to forget, if only for a little while, life's great tragedies, and heartaches, and sorrows; if you mean that drink, the sale of which pours into our treasuries untold millions of dollars, which are used to provide tender care for our little crippled children, our blind, our deaf, our dumb, our pitiful aged and infirm; to build highways and hospitals and schools, then certainly I am for it.

This is my stand. I will not retreat from it. I will not compromise.

**Photograph** courtesy The University of Mississippi Law School

# HOLT COLLIER

MARKSMAN

Holt Collier, born into slavery, demonstrated extraordinary marksmanship with the rifle. At the age of 10, he killed his first black bear (one of 3,000 he would kill in his lifetime). At the outbreak of the Civil War, Collier's owner set him free, but Collier joined the Confederate Army.

Collier was widely regarded as the best bear hunter in the South. In 1903, he served as the guide for Teddy Roosevelt's annual bear hunt. Collier captured a wounded bear and tied it to a tree. When Roosevelt refused to shoot the tethered animal, the story spread across the nation, leading to the "teddy bear" craze.

**Photograph** by Willa Johnson • Courtesy Minor Ferris Buchanan

# PARKER PICKLE

ONE OF A KIND

Parker Pickle. An incomparable name — and man.

He hides behind no pretense. His off-color stories will have you on the floor. A man told him a few years back that he cussed too much. Parker answered with a string of expletives that left the man speechless — all this while Parker was campaigning for Desoto County tax assessor. Cowering to no one, he's managed to be re-elected to the office for five consecutive terms.

Raised in Love, Mississippi on his family's dairy farm — the youngest of eight children — Parker carries a deep sense of family . . . and a deep-seated suspicion his father is waiting in hell for him with a list of unfinished chores.

Parker's sense of humor is only exceeded by his generosity. Friends and colleagues know you don't turn down an invitation to Parker's home, The Cedars. You'll never laugh so hard or enjoy such a delectable meal.

**Photograph and Story** by Karen Ott Mayer

# JOHN LESLIE

MAYOR, PHARMACIST

**"Mayor Leslie...dispenses pills, politics and pleasantries like a poultice."**

*Fred Brown, Memphis Press-Scimitar*

Author Willie Morris simply called him, "Your Worship."

Mayor of Oxford for 24 years, John Leslie was also the owner of the local pharmacy, Leslie's Drugs. The drug store was the place to be. The men stationed at coffee booths reminisced and gossiped. Leslie once prevented a fight between William Winter and Porter Fortune, who had locked themselves in his pharmacy office, while the White House was calling the front desk. As mayor, Leslie entertained dignitaries and celebrities passing through town. *Sophie's Choice* author William Styron once introduced himself publicly as "John Leslie's Speech Writer."

Leslie would regale friends, family or strangers for hours with his tales about Oxford. "Storytelling is a way of life here," he said.

In the Navy, as a signalman, Leslie was swapping jokes with a signalman on another boat when his commanding officer told him to stop. Wanting to get the last word, Leslie sent a final message telling the other signalman to kiss his derriere (though he shortened it to: KMA). When his commanding officer asked what the message meant, Leslie quipped, "It means 'keep me advised,' sir."

**Photograph** Mayor John Leslie (left) and Tommy Lee Jones (right) on location in Oxford for filming of Faulkner's *Barn Burning*.
Photo courtesy the Leslie family

# MOTEE DANIELS

### BOOTLEGGER, ENTREPRENEUR

orn in the rural community of Dog Town, Motee Daniels was known as an Oxford raconteur and, most famously, "bootlegger to William Faulkner." He knew poverty and hard work as a child, traveling by train to Arkansas each fall to pick cotton. He often remarked, "I got my Ph.D. in Dog Town, and it's worth three or four from Yale."

One of the highlights of political life in Lafayette County was Motee's run for the office of coroner-ranger. During the campaign, candidates gathered at the courthouse to deliver their speeches, and Motee appeared with his campaign manager — a talking dog named Buster. Buster sported a sign on his back that said "Motee Daniels for Coroner-Ranger. He's the same coming as going." There were two accompanying photos; one showed Motee from the front, the other from the back.

As a young man, Motee worked on road-building crews, hauled firewood, and picked cotton. Later, as a businessman, he traded successfully in land, mules, and real estate, and he operated a general store and roadhouse before retiring. The Lucille and Motee Daniels Award now honors the best scholastic papers delivered by Southern Studies graduate students as selected by a faculty committee.

Not bad for a Ph.D. from Dog Town.

**Photograph** courtesy Gene Gathright

# JOHN NELSON
TRAIN ENTHUSIAST

Combining an interest in old steam engines and old Delta logging railroads with a little determination and creativity, Panola County native John Nelson built his own Nelson Mills Railroad in his back yard. A short track, the railroad provides Nelson and visitors with a trip to the past on a real steam locomotive (named Marie) powered by a wood-fired engine.

**Photograph** courtesy *The Panolian*

# JACKIE SHERRILL

## COACH, MOTIVATOR

Y̲ou can't please everyone. This should be Jackie Sherrill's motto. He's been called "the cheatingest SOB in football," by Barry Switzer, and Joe Paterno once said he wouldn't retire and leave college football to "the Barry Switzers and Jackie Sherrills of the world." But opinions of Sherrill aren't all bad. When Sherrill became the head football coach at Mississippi State University, he led the team to 75 wins and six bowl games (prior to Sherrill's leadership, the team had only been to seven bowl games in 96 years). Ray Berryhill, the Mississippi State Director of Athlete Academics in 1991, said, "I think Coach Sherrill is committed to doing the best he can, and doing it the right way." Whether people love or hate him, it can't be denied that he did everything he could to motivate his team. Before a game against the then-number-13 Texas Longhorns, he famously castrated a bull during practice. Unranked Mississippi State went on to win the game.

**Photograph:** Mississippi State coach Jackie Sherrill in action during the Southwestern Bell Cotton Bowl against the Texas Longhorns.
Photo by Brian Bahr/Getty Images

# PAUL MCLEOD

ELVIS FAN

Paul McLeod turned his two-story home in Holly Springs into a shrine to Elvis Presley. Mississippians know it as "Graceland Too." The house is open to the public 24 hours a day, every day of the year. Though McLeod does charge a small fee for admittance, if you visit three times, you become a lifetime member of Graceland Too and subsequent visits are free. McLeod may hold the world's largest collection of Elvis paraphernalia, and if you catch him in the right mood, he may belt out an Elvis tune or two. Renowned for his reverence for Elvis (he named his son Elvis Aaron Presley Mcleod), McLeod claims to drink at least 24 soft drinks per day.

According to city officials, McLeod and his Graceland Too are Holly Springs' number one tourism attraction.

**Photograph** courtesy Michael Stanton

# RONZO SHAPIRO

MINISTER OF CULTURE

In 1975, a smitten "Ronzo" Shapiro followed an Ole Miss coed to Oxford where, after the romance faded, he stayed, and he and a group of carpenter friends built the Hoka. The business, a rustic, cinema-cum-coffeehouse, was named for Lafayette County's last Chickasaw princess. The converted cotton warehouse, a block off the town square, sported a tin roof and a sloping floor that Shapiro appointed with scavenged seats and a "rats-in-the-attic" décor. The Hoka became an unlikely gathering place for artists, musicians, and writers, as well as sorority girls, athletes, professors, Bible study groups and just plain folks. Shapiro has since become Oxford's unofficial "Minister of Culture." Through his campaigns for various local political offices, his ideas — including historic preservation, zoning, recycling, and public transportation — have all been implemented in 21st century Oxford.

Shapiro currently operates Main Squeeze, a gourmet juice/snack bar on University Avenue in Oxford. On pleasant nights, he shows movies in his parking lot to a whole new generation. Asked about his future plans, he gives his best 1960s "whatever" shrug and responds with a riddle — "Indecision may or may not be my problem."

**Photograph** courtesy Michael Stanton

# BOYCE HOLLEMAN

ATTORNEY, POLITICIAN, WAR VETERAN, ACTOR

Attorney, politician, war veteran, and actor, Jesse Boyce Holleman lived to help — and entertain — others. He was shot down in World War II during a bombing mission and was later awarded the Purple Heart. As a district attorney on the Mississippi Coast, Holleman survived an assassination attempt by the Dixie Mafia. He was re-elected to the office five times (a colleague once noted, "If you don't want to vote for Boyce, don't go listen to him speak.").

Holleman's courtroom brilliance and humor were legendary (when smoking in courtrooms was still allowed, Holleman would insert a straightened paper clip in the end of his cigar so his ever-growing ashes would make the perfectly-timed distraction).

Holleman launched an acting career when he was 51 years old. His one-man Clarence Darrow show garnered critical acclaim nationally. He performed on stage, television, and film; he had a starring role in the film adaptation of Eudora Welty's *The Ponder Heart* (his co-star was JoBeth Williams); and he remained an active member of the Screen Actors Guild. He once shared with a friend the secret to his acting success: "When you forget your lines, look at the other guy so the audience will think it was him!"

Boyce Holleman as Clarence Darrow. **Photograph** courtesy Michael Holleman

**Editor & Publisher**
Neil W. White, III

**Associate Editor**
Genie Leslie

**Associate Editor Photography**
Elizabeth Dollarhide

**Contributing Editors**
Louis Bourgeois, Julie Cantrell, Betsy Chapman, Pamela Massey, Margaret Seicshnaydre, Maggie White

**Contributing Photographers**
Kevin Bain, Maude Schuyler Clay, Langdon Clay, Houston Cofield, Tom Davis, Bill Ferris, Christopher Harris, Robert Jordan,  Nathan Latil, Mike Stanton, Ken Murphy, Bruce Newman, Milly Moorhead West, Jimmy Winstead

**Contributing Writers**
Ace Atkins, Louis Bourgois, Julie Cantrell, Jim Dees, Beth Ann Fennelly, Tom Franklin,
Jere Hoar, Kate Hooper, Richard Howorth, Mary Margaret White, Neil White

The publisher would like to thank the following groups and individuals:

Elizabeth Payne
Stella Connell
John Evans & Joe Hickman
Jim Ebel
The Margaret Alexander Walker Center, Jackson State University
Michael Rubenstein & The Mississippi Sports Hall of Fame & Museum
Mississippi Business Journal
Mississippi Department of History and Archives
The University of Mississippi Photographic Services
Nancy Jacobs, Director, The Mississippi Writers and Musicians Project
Corbis
Getty Images, and
James L. Cox's *The Mississippi Almanac*

We are also indebted to our corporate partners without whom this project would not have been possible.

Magnolia State Bank
The Olen Bailey Firm
Abraham's Department Store
The Baptist Memorial Hospital System
The Vicksburg Convention and Visitors Bureau
The Flowood Chamber of Commerce
Vector Transport
Venture Tech
Pearl River Resort Casino
Reed's GumTree Books
Lemuria Books
Square Books
Turnrow Books
Lorelei Books
Main Street Books
Barnes & Noble
Books-a-Million
and

All the Mississippians who nominated their favorite native sons and daughters.